APOLOGETICS QUOTES

Words That Will Strengthen Your Faith & Equip
You To Answer Critics of the Bible

CHARLIE H. CAMPBELL

For my beloved Lord and Savior Jesus,
& all those followers of His who desire to
be "ready to make a defense to every
one who asks" (1 Peter 3:15)

APOLOGETICS QUOTES
Words That Will Strengthen Your Faith & Equip You To Answer Critics of the Bible

Second Edition, Copyright © 2020. First edition © 2018.
by Charles H. Campbell

Published by The Always Be Ready Apologetics Ministry
P. O. Box 130342 Carlsbad CA 92013
Email: ABR@AlwaysBeReady.com

Additional copies of this book can be found at **AlwaysBeReady.com.**

All rights reserved. No portion of this book may be reproduced in any form without written permission from Charles Campbell or The Always Be Ready Apologetics Ministry.

ISBN: 978-1979800266

Cover graphic "Read in Peace" is from depositphotos.com.
Used by permission.

Printed in the United States of America.

Introduction

I love a clear, concise, helpful quote—especially when it addresses a challenging question or objection raised by critics of Christianity. Atheists and critics of the Bible bring up a variety of objections to the gospel that many Christians, unfortunately, are not well-prepared to respond to. Critics say:

- There's no evidence God exists!
- A loving God would not allow evil and suffering!
- The Bible was written by men—it's not trustworthy!
- Evolution has disproved the Bible!
- The Bible promotes war, slavery, and genocide!
- There's no good evidence that Jesus ever existed!
- A God of love would never send anyone to Hell!

If you've tried sharing the gospel with friends, family members, or coworkers, I'm sure you've heard some of these objections. How do you feel your responses went? Were you prepared to give an answer?

If you could use some help responding to these kinds of objections, I think you're going to love this book. It has more than 500 of my favorite apologetics quotes by many of the world's leading Christian apologists, men like:

- Norman Geisler
- Josh McDowell
- Lee Strobel
- Ravi Zacharias
- Tim Keller
- C.S. Lewis
- John Lennox
- J. Warner Wallace
- William Craig
- Frank Turek

Before you dive in, let me share a few quick things about the book's format that will help you get the most out of it.

First, the quotes are not arranged in specific categories. Many of the quotes would fit into more than one category. That would require duplication and a thicker book. So, instead, I've included a subject, person, and verse index in the back of the book. Take a quick peek at it. It should allow you to quickly find quotes on whatever subject you'd like to find.

Second, like authors of other quotes books, I decided to leave out the original source information for the quotes. If you are interested in finding the source details, do an Internet search with a snippet of the quote in quotation marks.

Third, I was persuaded to include some of my own quotes in this book. Several quotes of mine can be found circulating on Instagram and Facebook, and it appears that some of them were well-liked. So, I included some of the more popular ones. Forgive me if this seems presumptuous. I assure you that I don't think of myself in the same league as any of the great apologists featured in this book!

Fourth, you will notice in the book that some authors capitalize words like Heaven and Hell, and others do not. Some capitalize personal pronouns when referring to God, and others do not. I've tried to leave the authors' preferences in place. I hope you won't mind the inconsistency. I've also left the authors' punctuation preferences unchanged unless there was an obvious typo. So, you will probably notice a few places where you'd prefer to see a comma or semicolon. Keep in mind that some of these quotes were posted on Twitter and

Facebook, where the author wasn't as careful with punctuation as he would have been if he was writing a book.

Fifth, and finally, please don't take an author's inclusion in this book to mean that I endorse what the person may have said or written elsewhere. Some of the quotes in this book are by Christians who hold to different positions than you and me about debatable, non-essential doctrines of theology, for example, the order of end time events, the age of the Earth, etc. Don't squander precious time writing to me to say, "I was disappointed to see a quote in the book by so and so. Don't you know he believes ____?" Yes, I probably do know. But that doesn't mean his quote on something we agree upon isn't helpful. I've also included a handful of quotes in the book by Charles Darwin, and other agnostics and atheists because the quotes reveal something that lends support to a Christian perspective. Or I think their words offer an interesting insight into the lack of evidence for their agnostic or atheistic viewpoint.

Anyhow, enough of these kinds of details—grab a cup of tea or coffee, a pencil, and a highlighter, and enjoy reading.

Charlie Campbell
July 2, 2020
Southern California

APOLOGETICS QUOTES

"Apologetics must be motivated first, by the love of God, and second, by our love for our neighbor." –**Andy Bannister**

"When people question the Bible, don't take it personally, and try not to get defensive. God welcomes legitimate inquiry—in fact, He commands it: 'Test everything that is said. Hold on to what is good (1 Thess. 5:21).'" –**Mark Mittelberg**

"Certainly, there have been earlier ages when the culture was more sympathetic toward Christianity. But I think it's indisputable that there has never been a time in history when the hard evidence of science was more confirmatory of belief in God than today."
–**William Craig**

"The task of apologetics begins with a single person—you. A great thinker once said, 'Let him that would move the world first move himself.'" –**Ron Rhodes**

"You don't have to know everything before you start talking about something." –**Greg Koukl**

"If our culture is to be transformed, it will happen from the bottom up from ordinary believers practicing apologetics over the backyard fence or around the barbecue grill. To be sure, it's important for Christian scholars to conduct research and hold academic symposia, but the real leverage for cultural change comes from transforming the habits and dispositions of ordinary people." –**Charles Colson**

"We're not asking people to believe what the Bible says about God, just "because it says so." No. We want people to believe the Bible because of the wealth of good evidence that has demonstrated the Bible to be trustworthy...hundreds of fulfilled prophecies...thousands of archaeological discoveries...numerous details in the Bible that have been corroborated by extrabiblical historical sources, and so on." –**Charlie Campbell**

"Why don't the names of Buddha, Mohammed, Confucius offend people? The reason is that these others didn't claim to be God, but Jesus did." –**Josh McDowell**

"Natural selection may be able to explain the survival of a species, but it cannot explain the arrival of a species." –**Norman Geisler**

"I am persuaded that men think there is no God because they wish there were none. They find it hard to believe in God, and to go on in sin, so they try to get an easy conscience by denying his existence."
–**Charles Spurgeon**

"Looking at the doctrine of Darwinism, which undergirded my atheism for so many years, it didn't take me long to conclude that it was simply too far-fetched to be credible. I realized that if I were to embrace Darwinism and its underlying premise of naturalism, I would have to believe that: 1. Nothing produces everything 2. Non-life produces life 3. Randomness produces fine-tuning 4. Chaos produces information 5. Unconsciousness produces consciousness 6. Non-reason produces reason...The central pillars of evolutionary theory quickly rotted away when exposed to scrutiny." –**Lee Strobel**

"Men do not reject the Bible because it contradicts itself, but because it contradicts them." –E. Paul Hovey

"It is absurd for the evolutionists to complain that it's unthinkable for an admittedly unthinkable God to make everything out of nothing and then pretend it is more thinkable that nothing should turn itself into anything." –**G.K. Chesterton**

"Christianity, if false, is of no importance, and, if true, of infinite importance. The one thing it cannot be is moderately important."
–**C.S. Lewis**

"People are free to accept or reject what Scripture says. What they are not free to do is to claim it says something it does not. In modern times that's called "spin." In an earlier time, it was called heresy."
–**Cal Thomas**

"I can see how it might be possible for a man to look down upon earth and be an atheist, but I cannot conceive how he could look up into the heavens and say that there is no God."
–**Abraham Lincoln**

"All religions and philosophies say, 'This is the way.' Only Jesus says, 'I am the Way.'" –**Tim Keller**

"The Bible is not such a book a man would write if he could, or could write if he would." –**Lewis Sperry Chafer**

"Discoveries of the last half of the 20th century have brought the scientific community to the realization that our universe and our planet in the universe are so remarkably unique that it is almost impossible to imagine how this could have happened accidentally, causing many agnostic scientists to concede that indeed some intelligent creative force may be required to account for it." –**Walter Bradley**

"There are more sure marks of authenticity in the Bible than in any profane [secular] history." –**Isaac Newton**

"The believer in God must explain one thing, the existence of sufferings; the nonbeliever, however, must explain the existence of everything else." –**Dennis Prager**

"When someone tells me 'We can't trust the Bible because it was written by men,' I like to gently point out that their conclusion doesn't follow their premise. Just because something was written by men doesn't mean it's not trustworthy. If that were the case we would have to throw out encyclopedias, dictionaries, automobile manuals, et cetera—all written by men. Men are capable of communicating truthfully, especially when they have God's help, as the Biblical authors did." –**Charlie Campbell**

"There are only two kinds of religion in the world...They all say, "Do, do, do." Only Christianity says, "Done." Christ has done it all."
–**J. Vernon McGee**

"The rule that science is the only way to know something is itself unscientific; it cannot be tested. So the claim that only science can demonstrate truth actually flunks its own test, since it cannot validate itself!" –**Gary Habermas**

"I know the resurrection is a fact, and Watergate proved it to me. How? Because 12 men testified they had seen Jesus raised from the dead, then they proclaimed that truth for 40 years, never once denying it. Every one was beaten, tortured, stoned and put in prison. They would not have endured that if it weren't true. Watergate embroiled 12 of the most powerful men in the world—and they couldn't keep a lie for three weeks. You're telling me 12 apostles could keep a lie for 40 years? Absolutely impossible." –**Charles Colson**

"The Old Testament contains over 300 references to the Messiah that were fulfilled in Jesus Christ. Computations using the science of probability on just 8 of these prophecies show the chance that someone could have fulfilled all 8 prophecies is 10 (to the 17th power), or 1 in 100 quadrillion." –**Fritz Ridenour**

"Human DNA contains more organized information than the *Encyclopedia Britannica*. If the full text of the encyclopedia were to arrive in computer code from outer space, most people would regard this as proof of the existence of extraterrestrial intelligence. But when seen in nature, it is explained [by Darwinists] as the workings of random forces." –**George Sim Johnson**

"Every religion in the world except one says you must work your way to God. Only Biblical Christianity says God has worked His way to you." –**Ed Hindson**

"Christians believe in the virgin birth of Jesus. Materialists believe in the virgin birth of the cosmos. Choose your miracle."
–**Glen Scrivener**

"If the truth offends, then let it offend. People have been living their whole lives in offense to God; let them be offended for a while."
–**John MacArthur**

"To be an atheist you must have infinite knowledge in order to know absolutely that there is no God. But to have infinite knowledge, you would have to be God yourself. It's hard to be God yourself and an atheist at the same time! The Bible says in Psalm 14:1, "The fool says in his heart, 'There is no God.'" –**Ron Carlson** and **Ed Decker**

"The Biblical worldview is the only one that accepts the reality of evil and suffering while giving both the cause and the purpose, while offering God–given strength and sustenance in the midst of it."
–**Ravi Zacharias**

"A lot of the time people aren't on a truth quest, they are on a happiness quest. But the only way to get ultimate happiness is to go through truth." –**Frank Turek**

"If the Bible is not the Word of God and inspired, the whole of Christendom for 1800 years has been under an immense delusion; half the human race has been cheated and deceived, and churches are monuments of folly. If the Bible is the Word of God and inspired, all who refuse to believe it are in fearful danger; they are living on the brink of eternal misery. No man, in his sober senses, can fail to see that the whole subject demands most serious attention." –**J.C. Ryle**

"Saying you're a new kind of Christian with a new kind of Christianity is basically saying you're an old kind of heretic." –**Burk Parsons**

"If we had absolute proof instead of clues, then you could no more deny God than you could deny the sun. If we had no evidence at all, you could never get there. God gives us just enough evidence so that those who want Him can have Him." –**Peter Kreeft**

"There is no neutral ground when it comes to the tolerance question. Everybody has a point of view she thinks is right, and everybody passes judgment at some point or another. The Christian gets pigeonholed as the judgmental one, but everyone else is judging, too, even people who consider themselves relativists." –**Greg Koukl**

"Merely having an open mind is nothing; the object of opening the mind, as of opening the mouth, is to shut it again on something solid." –**G.K. Chesterton**

"Cults use our vocabulary, but they don't use our dictionary."
–**Charles Swindoll**

"Infidels, with all their assaults, make about as much impression on this book as a man with a tack hammer would on the Pyramids of Egypt. When the French monarch proposed the persecution of the Christians in his dominion, an old statesman and warrior said to him, 'Sire, the Church of God is an anvil that has worn out many hammers.' So the hammers of infidels have been pecking away at this book for ages, but the hammers are worn out, and the anvil still endures." –**H.L. Hastings**

"Indeed, faith is a response to evidence, not a rejoicing in the absence of evidence." –**John Lennox**

"Donald Page of Princeton's Institute for Advanced Science calculated the odds against our universe randomly taking a form suitable for life as one in: $10,000,000,000^{124}$. That's one in ten billion to the 124th power! I'm not sure how far along you got in your mathematics studies in high school or college, but I think you could agree with me that these are such astronomical odds, it is reasonable to conclude that the universe did not end up with these finely-tuned conditions apart from an incredibly intelligent and powerful designer."
–**Charlie Campbell**

"While Western atheists turn from belief in God because a tsunami in another part of the world caused great suffering, many broken-hearted survivors of that same tsunami found faith in God. This is one of the great paradoxes of suffering. Those who don't suffer much think suffering should keep people from God, while many who suffer a great deal turn to God, not from him." –**Randy Alcorn**

"If God would concede me His omnipotence for 24 hours, you would see how many changes I would make in the world. But if He gave me His wisdom too, I would leave things as they are." –**J.M.L. Monsabre**

"If Christianity was something we were making up, of course we could make it easier. But it is not. We cannot compete, in simplicity, with people who are inventing religions. How could we? We are dealing with Fact. Of course anyone can be simple if he has no facts to bother about." –**C.S. Lewis**

"Neanderthal man turned out to be not an ape-man but rather truly human. Java man turned out to be an arboreal ape. Piltdown man turned out to be a colossal hoax. Peking man turned out to be a monkey. Nebraska man turned out to be a wild pig. Lucy was apparently a chimpanzee. Yet, in each case, when these discoveries were made, the popular media reported them as hard proof for evolutionary theory." –**Ron Rhodes**

"I really believe we're on the cusp of a golden era in Christian apologetics. We're living in very exciting times. The water has been stirred

by atheists, anti-theists and agnostics, and there's an atmosphere of skepticism because of it. To me, that just spells opportunity; it means people are thinking about these issues, and they're willing to listen and engage and discuss these topics. ==Apologetics has always been the handmaiden of evangelism.== It's a tool that's used in the evangelistic process. It's always about helping people get past those spiritual sticking points that are holding them up in their spiritual journeys."
–**Lee Strobel**

"The chief reason people do not know God is not because He hides from them but because they hide from Him." –**John Stott**

"Alexander, Caesar, Charlemagne, and myself founded empires; but upon what foundation did we rest the creations of our genius? Upon force! But Jesus Christ founded His upon love; and at this hour millions of men would die for Him." –**Napoleon Bonaparte I**

"A well-known scientist, a very decorated scientist named Herbert Spencer died in 1903. In his scientific career he had become noted for one great discovery, it was a categorical contribution that he made. He discovered that all reality, all that exists in the universe can be contained in five categories: time, force, action, space and matter. Herbert Spencer said everything that exists, exists in one of those categories: time, force, action, space and matter. Nothing exists outside of those categories. That was a very astute discovery and didn't come until the nineteenth century. Now think about that. Spencer even listed them in that order: time, force, action, space and matter. That is a logical sequence. And then with that in your mind, listen to Genesis 1:1. "In the beginning (that's time), God (that's force) created (that's action) the heavens (that's space) and the earth (that's matter)." In the first verse of the Bible God said plainly what man didn't catalog until the nineteenth century. Everything that could be said about everything that exists is said in that first verse."
–**John MacArthur**

"Ronald Reagan once quipped, "I've noticed all those in favor of abortion are already born." Indeed, all pro-abortionists would become pro-life immediately if they found themselves back in the womb." –**Norman Geisler**

"After more than two centuries of facing the heaviest scientific guns that could be brought to bear, the Bible has survived—and is perhaps the better for the siege. Even on the critics' own terms—historical fact—the Scriptures seem more acceptable now than they did when the rationalists began the attack." –**TIME Magazine**

"Where in all the world could sixty-six books be collected from more than forty authors, be written over a period of more than sixteen hundred years, and yet form one united and continual presentation of divine truth? If the Bible is not inspired of God, it would be a greater miracle than its own inspiration. The unity of Scripture is one of the convincing evidences that the Bible is not a natural book, but a book which God Himself directed and produced through human authors." –**John Walvoord**

"The fact that the Christian fellowship, founded on belief in Jesus' resurrection, could come into existence and flourish in the very city where he was executed and buried seems to be compelling evidence for the historicity of the empty tomb." –**William Craig**

"The god of Islam requires followers to die for him. The God I serve sent His Son Jesus Christ to die for me and you." –**Franklin Graham**

"Just as bank tellers need a thorough knowledge of legitimate currency in order to spot counterfeit bills, so Christians need a thorough knowledge of the Bible in order to spot bogus religious teachings. How grounded are you in the Scriptures? How deep are your theological roots? How capable are you of detecting false teachings?" –**Charles Swindoll**

"There are only two kinds of people in the end: those who say to God, 'Thy will be done,' and those to whom God says, in the end, 'Thy will be done.'" –**C.S. Lewis**

"I don't believe in Christianity because it makes me feel good (often it doesn't), but for one reason: because it is true." –**Andy Bannister**

"It always amuses me that atheists often argue for the existence of extra-terrestrial intelligence beyond earth. Yet they are only too eager to denounce the possibility that we already have a vast, intelligent being out there: God." –**John Lennox**

"For some people, God is an old man with a beard sitting on a throne out in space somewhere. If that's the kind of God they don't believe in, then I agree with them." –**Greg Koukl**

"Archaeological work has unquestionably strengthened confidence in the reliability of the Scriptural record. More than one archaeologist has found his respect for the Bible increased by the experience of excavation in Palestine." –**Millar Burrows**

"If one believes in the existence of Socrates, Alexander the Great, or Julius Caesar, then one should definitely believe in Christ's existence. If historicity is established by written records in multiple copies that date originally from near contemporaneous sources, there is far more historical evidence for Christ's existence than for any of theirs. The historicity of Christ is attested not only by Christians but also by Greek, Roman, and Jewish Sources." –**Josh McDowell** and **Dave Sterrett**

"We shouldn't love people in order to share our faith with them. Rather, we share our faith and ourselves with them in order to love them." –**Tim Keller**

"No other book in the world is able to substantiate its claims with this kind of supernatural ability to rightly foretell future events. There are no fulfilled prophecies in the Quran, the Hindu Vedas, the Book of Mormon, or any other sacred religious writings. Not one. Fulfilled prophecy is something that sets the Bible apart from every other religious book." –**Charlie Campbell**

"Don't merely make the case that Christianity is true. Make the case that it is good and beautiful." –**Sean McDowell**

"He who reads the Bible to find fault with it will soon discover that the Bible finds fault with him." –**Charles Spurgeon**

"If all we need is a teacher of enlightenment, the Buddha will do; if all we need is a collection of gods for every occasion and need and hope, Hinduism will do; if all we need is a tribal deity, any tribal deity will do; if all we need is a lawgiver, Moses will do; if all we need is a set of rules and a way of devotion, Muhammad or Joseph Smith will do; if all we need is inspiration and insight into the sovereign self, Oprah will do; but if we need a savior, only Jesus will do."
–**Albert Mohler**

"If there is a God who can act, then there can be acts of God. The only way to show that miracles are impossible is to disprove the existence of God." –**Norman Geisler**

"Many today seem blissfully unaware that they are using self-defeating arguments when expressing their commitment to relativistic truth. The Christian can debunk such sloppy thinking by asking some logical questions: If they say, "There are no absolutes," you can respond, "Are you absolutely sure about that?" If they say, "We cannot be certain about anything," you can respond, "Are you certain about that?" If they say, "We should doubt everything," you can respond, "Should that statement be doubted?" If they say, "We cannot know truth," you can respond, "How do you know that is true?" If they say, "We should never judge," you can respond, "If it is wrong to judge, then why are you judging?" If they say, "It is true for you but not for me," you can respond, "Is that statement just true for you but not for me?" If they say, "Truth about God is not objective," you can respond, "Is that an objective truth about God?" If they say, "Words cannot express meaning," you can respond, "Do those words express meaning?" If they say, "There is no rational support for what we believe," you can respond, "Is there any rational support for that belief?" –**Ron Rhodes**

"Despite the horrors the Canaanites were committing, the new atheists complain that God was immoral for stopping them. Yet on nearly every college campus I visit, an atheist declares, "If there is a good God, He would intervene to stop evil in the world." Well, here is a case where God does intervene, and the atheists are complaining about it!" –**Frank Turek**

"I believe in Christianity as I believe that the sun has risen, not only because I see it, but because by it I see everything else." –**C.S. Lewis**

"The Gospel is not true because it works; the Gospel works because it is true." –**Andy Bannister**

"I am glad there are things in the Bible I do not understand. If I could take that book up and read it as I would any other book, I might think I could write a book like that." –**Dwight L. Moody**

"Again and again throughout history, the archaeological evidence has supported the biblical record, not contradicted it. The evidence is clearly on the side of the Bible. Be wary of the latest news story claiming to debunk some key aspect of Christianity on the basis of recent findings that have yet to be studied in detail by qualified scholars." –**Robert Velarde**

Scholar and apologist R.C. Sproul was once asked, "What is the difference between the Christian God, and the gods of the other religions?" He simply, yet profoundly answered, "The main difference is this: The God of Christianity exists." –**R.C. Sproul**

"We are called to be earnest contenders for the faith. This is not a call to be contentious, mean-spirited, or looking for an argument. "And the servant of the Lord must not quarrel but be gentle to all, able to teach, patient, in humility correcting those who are in opposition, if God will perhaps grant them repentance, so that they may know the truth" (2 Timothy 2:24–25). We must speak the truth in love (Ephesians 4:15). Harsh, unloving use of the truth of God is not edifying to man or glorifying to God." –**Bob Hoekstra**

"I'm not a Christian because it "works" for me. I had a life prior to Christianity that seemed to be working just fine, and my life as a Christian hasn't always been easy. I'm a Christian because it is true. I'm a Christian because I want to live in a way that reflects the truth. I'm a Christian because my high regard for the truth leaves me no alternative." –**J. Warner Wallace**

"That's the biggest problem for evolution: how life got started. Because you need DNA to make proteins, you need DNA to make RNA, and you need RNA to make proteins. So, it's worse than 'what came first, the chicken or the egg?'" –**Jeff Tomkins**

"As a child I received instruction both in the Bible and in the Talmud. I am a Jew, but I am enthralled by the luminous figure of the Nazarene...No one can read the Gospels without feeling the actual presence of Jesus. His personality pulsates in every word. No myth is filled with such life." –**Albert Einstein**

"It comes as no shock to those who have been following trends in the church and our culture to hear that young people—especially Millennials—are leaving the church in great numbers...one major issue is a lack of apologetics teaching. Millennials have not been taught to defend their faith against the secular attacks of our day, and the scoffing and arguments of the secular world have drawn them away." –**Ken Ham**

"God created the possibility of evil; people actualized that potentiality. The source of evil is not God's power but mankind's freedom. Even an all-powerful God could not have created a world in which people had genuine freedom and yet there was no potentiality for sin, because our freedom includes the possibility of sin within its own meaning." –**Peter Kreeft**

"I feel no hesitation in avowing, that I believe in the plenary inspiration of every word of the original text of Holy Scripture. I hold not only that the Bible contains the Word of God, but that every jot of it was written, or brought together, by Divine inspiration, and is the Word of God. I entirely disagree with those who maintain that the writers of the Bible were partially inspired, or inspired to such a limited extent that discrepancies, inaccuracies, and contradictions to the facts of science and history, must be expected and do exist in their writings. I utterly repudiate such a theory. I consider that it practically destroys the whole value of God's Word, puts a sword in the hand of infidels and skeptics, and raises far more serious difficulties than it pretends to solve." –**J.C. Ryle**

"No one alive today would believe that the faces of Mount Rushmore came about by millions of years of erosion, wind, rain, and undirected random acts. And yet atheists believe that real–life human beings with 206 bones, about 700 muscles, and hearts that beat over 100,000 times a day are the product of a mindless, random series of accidents and mutations—mutations that have never been shown to add any information to the human genetic code. Well, I don't have enough faith to believe that." –**Charlie Campbell**

"If you say you don't believe in God but you do believe in the rights of every person and the requirement to care for all the weak and the poor, then you are still holding on to Christian beliefs, whether you will admit it or not. Why, for example, should you look at love and aggression—both parts of life, both rooted in our human nature—and choose one as good and reject one as bad? They are both part of life. Where do you get a standard to do that? If there is no God or supernatural realm, it doesn't exist." –**Tim Keller**

"A failure to understand something does not mean it is irrational. It may simply mean that it lies on the far side of our limited abilities to take things in and make complete sense of them." –**Alister McGrath**

"One of the most bitter complaints of critics against the Bible is its portrayal of the severity of God, especially in His command to Moses to destroy all the Canaanites (Deuteronomy 7:2)...[But] God had given them 400 years to repent (Genesis), but each new generation had gone further away from God than the one before, and they were practicing (as archaeology has revealed) every form of debauchery known to man. It was an act of mercy by God toward all those who would come in contact with them in future generations to decree their destruction now. They had already irrevocably hardened their hearts toward God." –**Henry Morris**

"So to imagine that these dejected souls somehow concocted a plan to steal the body of the one who taught them never to steal, and then to tell lies about the one who taught them never to lie, all so they could be persecuted for the rest of their days while feigning a false hope over the return of their murdered Messiah...well, that stretches my mind beyond credulity." –**Lee Strobel**

"I've learned to distinguish between the greatness of God and the inexcusable evil that has been done by those professing his name. And so I do not deduce [as Christopher Hitchens does] that God is not great, and that religion poisons everything. After all, if I failed to distinguish between the genius of Einstein and the abuse of his science to create weapons of mass destruction, I might be tempted to say science is not great, and technology poisons everything."
–**John Lennox**

"If you are drawn into controversy, use very hard arguments and very soft words. Frequently you cannot convince a man by tugging at his reason, but you can persuade him by winning his affections."
–**Charles Spurgeon**

"The Bible constantly exhorts believers to beware of false prophets (Matt. 7:15), to test the spirits (1 John 4:1), and to watch out for the doctrines of demons (1 Timothy 4:1). But there is no way to recognize error unless we know the truth; counterfeits cannot be detected unless we know the genuine article. Likewise, there is no way to determine what is false about God unless we know what is true about him. Jesus said, "You will know the truth, and the truth will set you free" (John 8:32). A study of the attributes of the true God is essential to the fulfillment of the apologetic task of defending the faith (Philippians 1:7; 1 Peter 3:15; Jude 3)." –**Norman Geisler**

"We find fossils of sea creatures in rock layers that cover all the continents. For example, most of the rock layers in the walls of Grand Canyon (more than a mile above sea level) contain marine fossils. Fossilized shellfish are even found in the Himalayas."
–**Andrew Snelling**

"The Canadian scientist G.B. Hardy one time said, "When I looked at religion I said, I have two questions. One, has anybody ever conquered death, and two, if they have, did they make a way for me to conquer death? I checked the tomb of Buddha, and it was occupied, and I checked the tomb of Confucius and it was occupied, and I checked the tomb of Mohammed and it was occupied, and I came to the tomb of Jesus and it was empty. And I said, there is one who conquered death. And I asked the second question, did He make a way for me to do it? And I opened the Bible and discovered that He said, 'Because I live ye shall live also.'" –**John MacArthur**

"Since atheists are unable to coherently support materialism, the heart of their case for atheism boils down to complaints about the way God does things: 'If I were God, I wouldn't do it this way. I wouldn't allow evil. I would have designed things differently. I would write everyone's name in the sky.'...But complaints are not arguments. A teenager may complain about a set of instructions his father left behind—the kid may want to do things completely differently. But that's not an argument for the non-existence or malice of the father."
–**Frank Turek**

"Anyone with sincere religious beliefs cannot say that all religions are true. That is so illogical it is pathetic. All religion cannot be true because some of them are so diametrically opposed to each other."
–**Josh McDowell**

"You must know how to defend your own beliefs. If we cannot answer their genuine questions, we will "confirm" in their minds what they are often brainwashed into believing: that Christianity is intellectually flawed. This is what they are told. One doesn't need to have

all the answers, but one should know where they are found."
–**Ravi Zacharias**

"Jesus, unlike any other religious leader, proved He was the Son of God (and therefore a reliable source of information on eternity) by... fulfilling numerous Old Testament prophecies made hundreds of years in advance, performing numerous miracles, living a sinless life, His resurrection from the dead. When one considers these facts and the plethora of other evidences for the reliability of the Bible, a very strong case can be made as to why every thinking person should take Jesus's claims seriously." –**Charlie Campbell**

"If Christians could be trained to provide solid evidence for what they believe and good answers to unbelievers' questions and objections, then the perception of Christians would slowly change. Christians would be seen as thoughtful people to be taken seriously rather than as emotional fanatics or buffoons. The gospel would be a real alternative for people to embrace." –**William Craig**

"Christ remains the most influential figure in history. Any list of world-transforming individuals would no doubt include Moses, Buddha, and Muhammad. Moses, Buddha, and Muhammad, however occupy totally different places in Judaism, Buddhism, and Islam than Christ occupies in Christianity. Moses, Buddha, and Muhammad never professed to perform miracles; indeed they never claimed to be anything more than men. They viewed themselves simply as God's messengers. Christ is the only person in history who has defined a whole religion around his person." –**Dinesh D'Souza**

"Jesus accepted the plenary [i.e., complete, extending to all its parts] inspiration of the Bible; when first approached by the devil to turn stones into bread, our Lord replied that man lives by every word that proceeds from the mouth of God (Matt. 4:4 quoting Deut. 8:3). He did not say, "some words" but "every word." If Scripture is breathed out from God (2 Tim. 3:16), then Scripture must be included in what sustains man, not only parts of Scripture but all of it." –**Charles Ryrie**

"I believe that the damned are, in one sense, successful rebels to the end; that the doors of hell are locked on the *inside*." –**C.S. Lewis**

"God sends no one to hell. We send ourselves. God has done all that is necessary for us to be forgiven, redeemed, cleansed and made fit for heaven. All that remains is for us to receive this gift." –**Paul Little**

"Critiquing bad religion is not something that Christopher Hitchens first dreamt up as he sat down at his word processor one evening to bang out *God Is Not Great*. That religions sometimes can go badly wrong is a much older point, indeed one made some 2,000 years earlier by Jesus himself. His most frequent clashes were with the religious leaders of his day, whom he accused of using religion for personal gain, or as a tool to exploit and to marginalize. In short, if you're going to criticize religion when it goes wrong, you're probably closer to Jesus on that issue than you might ever have imagined."
–**Andy Bannister**

"As Christians, we don't just need answers for people's difficult questions. We need questions for people's easy answers."
–**Andrew Wilson**

"Always make it a goal to keep your conversations cordial. Sometimes that will not be possible. If a principled, charitable expression of your ideas makes someone mad, there's little you can do about it. Jesus' teaching made some people furious. Just make sure it's your ideas that offend and not you, that your beliefs cause the dispute and not your behavior." –**Greg Koukl**

"It may be stated categorically that no archaeological discovery has ever controverted a Biblical reference. Scores of archaeological findings have been made which confirm in clear outline or exact detail historical statements in the Bible. And, by the same token, proper evaluation of Biblical descriptions has often led to amazing discoveries." –**Nelson Glueck**

"As Christians, we may not always like where our faith demands that we stand, and yet, we must. Even so, civility need not be sacrificed on the altar of truth nor truth sacrificed on the altar of civility. Truth given in love is what our Savior demonstrated, and what He demanded from His Church." –**Sean McDowell**

"Evolutionists once claimed there were some one hundred eighty vestigial organs (with no known function) left over from our animal ancestry. Over the last century or so, this list has shrunk to six! And now there are known functions even for these." –**Norman Geisler**

"Jesus is mentioned by more than 30 sources outside the New Testament within 150 years of His life, including the Roman historians Tacitus and Suetonius, Flavius Josephus, and the Jewish Talmud...the claim that Jesus was just an invention by some clever deceivers 2000 years ago falters at every level." –**Charlie Campbell**

"Because Christ raised no doubts about the adequacy of the Scripture as His contemporaries knew them, we can safely assume that the first-century text of the Old Testament was a wholly adequate representation of the divine word originally given. Jesus regarded the extant copies of His day as so approximate to the originals in their message that He appealed to those copies as authoritative."
–**Greg Bahnsen**

"God permitted slavery to exist in both Old and New Testament times. But this does not mean that slavery was a God-ordained system. Slavery was an invention of fallen man—not of God. Nevertheless, God allowed it to exist the way He allows other things to exist that He does not approve of: murder, lying, rape, theft, etc...God worked within the fallen system of man and put limits and guidelines concerning the treatment of slaves." –**Matt Slick**

"Today, people continue to rebel against God. We curse Him, ignore Him, and flaunt our disobedience. Motivated by pride, greed, and selfishness, people destroy one another and willfully abuse and pollute God's earth...it's amazing God has not lost His patience and destroyed all of us. Rather than condemning God for allowing evil, we

should be thankful that He withholds the punishment we deserve."
–**Dan Story**

"People will die for their religious beliefs if they sincerely believe they're true, but people won't die for their religious beliefs if they know their beliefs are false. While most people can only have faith that their beliefs are true, the disciples were in a position to know without a doubt whether or not Jesus had risen from the dead. They claimed that they saw him, talked with him, and ate with him. If they weren't absolutely certain, they wouldn't have allowed themselves to be tortured to death for proclaiming that the Resurrection had happened." –**Lee Strobel**

"When this particular issue [homosexuality] is unaddressed by the church, it leaves room for many unbiblical opinions and immature conversations to fill in the blanks. Due to a lack of biblical knowledge and the silence of the church, people are confused, left to wonder, and end up making unhealthy decisions that can be very destructive to everyone. Leaving this issue unaddressed helps no one, and can end up hurting everyone. Every church must address homosexuality. And every church must use the Bible as its ultimate guide for wisdom, love, and truth." –**Landon Schott**

"The Devil can cite Scripture for his purpose."–**William Shakespeare**

"Ultimately, apologetics points people to our hope, Jesus Himself. That's why "we demolish arguments and every high-minded thing that is raised up against the knowledge of God, taking every thought captive to the obedience of Christ" (2 Corinthians 10:4–5). Objections raised against Jesus must be demolished. But notice something. The Bible doesn't say we demolish people. Rather we demolish arguments. Belittling others is not our goal. Merely winning arguments is not enough. Instead, we remove obstacles of doubt to Christianity so people can take a serious look at Christ, the only source of hope for this world." –**Brett Kunkle**

"As Christians, we are to have no dealings with the mythology of astrology. Astrology is an ancient belief that celestial spirits, planetary gods, and the movement and alignment of stars and planets affect day-to-day life. Christians have no sign; we've been delivered from these weak and ancient philosophies (Col. 2:8). We are led by the word of God and transformed by His Spirit. Zodiac signs are foolishness." –**Ronald Wright**

"Ever since scientific archaeology started a century and a half ago, the consistent pattern has been this: the hard evidence from the ground has borne out the biblical record again and again—and again. The Bible has nothing to fear from the spade." –**Paul Maier**

"Astronomers now find they have painted themselves into a corner because they have proven, by their own methods, that the world began abruptly in an act of creation to which you can trace the seeds of every star, every planet, every living thing in this cosmos and on the earth. And they have found that all this happened as a product of forces they cannot hope to discover. That there are what I or anyone would call supernatural forces at work is now, I think, a scientifically proven fact." –**Robert Jastrow**

"If the New Testament is historically reliable, then you get the Old Testament thrown in on the authority of Jesus. For if Jesus really is God, as the New Testament documents claim He is, then whatever God teaches is true. Jesus taught that the entire Old Testament is the Word of God." –**Frank Turek**

"Remember that you and I do not have the power in ourselves to convert anyone. That is God's job. You and I witness (Matthew 28:19–20; Acts 1:8); only our supernatural and miraculous God has the power to convert (see John 6:39–40,44)." –**Ron Rhodes**

"Now there were many attempts made by Satan to infiltrate the Old Testament Canon with uninspired books. At least 14 of them have been accumulated and together they are called the Apocrypha. You find them in a Roman Catholic Bible. They are not a part of our Bible. They are not inspired books….They were clearly fakes. How do we know they were fakes? They were written long after the canon was completed and they lacked the prophetic quality and authorship to stamp them as inspired Scripture. None of their writers claimed divine inspiration and some openly disclaimed it. And Apocrypha books contained errors of facts, errors of ethics, errors of doctrine. For example, some of the Apocrypha books advocate suicide. Some of them advocate assassination and some of them teach praying for dead people. Therein lies one of the reasons you find them in a Catholic Bible." –**John MacArthur**

"Atheists say, 'Why doesn't God just appear to us in a public setting and prove to the world He exists?' You mean like the time God came to the Earth in the person of Jesus, raised the dead, healed cripples, and opened the eyes of the blind, only to then be dragged away and nailed to a cross? My friend, God has already appeared publicly to humans. God knows that appearing to you publicly wouldn't change your heart. He knows that He's already provided enough evidence for His existence for those who truly want to know Him."
–**Charlie Campbell**

"The average Christian in the pew is not reading books by Richard Dawkins and Christopher Hitchens, but their neighbors and coworkers are. I think congregations are putting pressure on churches to equip them better, educate them more and give them opportunities to grow in this area. Churches that have relied in the past on a lifestyle evangelistic approach that lacks intentionality need to be a little more intentional in reaching people and bringing answers to their questions. I'm all for lifestyle evangelism, but I'm also in favor of intentionality, where we seek out opportunities for spiritual conversations and are equipped to explain the gospel and why we believe it." –**Lee Strobel**

"Long before scientists had discovered such data, many scientific facts had been recorded in Scripture. Among them include: The roundness of the earth (Isaiah 40:22), the law of conservation of mass and energy (2 Peter 3:7), the hydrologic cycle (Ecclesiastes 1:7), the vast number of stars (Jeremiah 33:22), the law of increasing entropy (Psalm 102:25-27), the importance of blood to life (Leviticus 17:11), atmospheric circulation (Ecclesiastes 1:6) The gravitational field (Job 26:7). The Bible is not a science textbook, but it does speak accurately when it notes aspects of the natural world. While the Bible does not explain all there is to know about the created world, it does offer an accurate description of our world, as well as the revelation needed to obtain salvation." –**Alex McFarland**

"I have noticed that whenever a person gives up his belief in the Word of God because it requires that he should believe a good deal, his unbelief requires him to believe a great deal more. If there be any difficulties in the faith of Christ, they are not one-tenth as great as the absurdities in any system of unbelief which seeks to take its place." –**Charles Spurgeon**

"As the fear of God is the beginning of wisdom, so the denial of God is the height of foolishness." –**R.C. Sproul**

"Most Christians, while unfamiliar with many of the technical arguments for the inspiration of the Bible, are convinced that the Bible is the Word of God because of what it has done in their own life. The influence of the Bible on millions of those who have put their trust in it is an attested fact of history. Those who have been moral wrecks and victims of drink and drugs have been marvelously redeemed through the power of the Word of God." –**John Walvoord**

"Let us remember that every worldview—not just Christianity's—must give an explanation or an answer for evil and suffering...this is not just a problem distinctive to Christianity. It will not do for the challenger just to raise the question. This problem of evil is one to which we all must offer an answer, regardless of the belief system to which we subscribe." –**Ravi Zacharias**

"For eighteen centuries every engine of destruction that human science, philosophy, wit, reasoning or brutality could bring to bear against a book has been brought to bear against that book to stamp it out of the world, but it has a mightier hold on the world today than ever before. If that were man's book it would have been annihilated and forgotten hundreds of years ago." –**R.A. Torrey**

"The excessive skepticism of many liberal theologians stems not from a careful evaluation of the available data, but from an enormous predisposition against the supernatural." –**Millar Burrows**

"If you want to look very wise in the world's eyes and are willing to risk looking foolish years from now, you can make a reputation for yourself by pointing out the "errors" in the Bible. But these things tend to become explained. As time passes and the data from archaeology, historical investigations, numismatics [coins], and other disciplines accumulate, these alleged "errors" tend to explode in the faces of those who propound them..." –**James Boice**

"Skeptics may mention biblical cities that haven't been discovered—though lots have been!—and conclude that Scripture is unreliable. But in the past "absence of evidence" arguments were used to deny the factuality of Abraham's camels, the Hittite people, and the Davidic dynasty. But with new discoveries in archaeology, the skeptics were proven wrong and Scripture was confirmed." –**Paul Copan**

"Because free will, though it makes evil possible, is also the only thing that makes possible any love or goodness or joy worth having." –**C.S. Lewis**

"For my own part, I believe that in dealing with skeptics, and unbelievers, and enemies of the Bible, Christians are too apt to stand only on the defensive. They are too often content with answering this or that little objection, or discussing this or that little difficulty, which is picked out of Scripture and thrown in their teeth. I believe we ought to act on the aggressive far more than we do, and to press home on the adversaries of [Biblical] inspiration the enormous difficulties of their own position." –**J.C. Ryle**

"Why then is not every geological formation and every stratum full of such intermediate links? Geology assuredly does not reveal any such finely graduated organic chain, and this, perhaps, is the most obvious and gravest objection which can be urged against my theory." –**Charles Darwin**

"As vital as it is for us to enlist in the Truth War and do battle for our faith, it is even more important to remember why we are fighting—not merely for the thrill of vanquishing some foe or winning some argument, but out of a genuine love for Christ, who is the living, breathing embodiment of all that we hold true and worth fighting for." –**John MacArthur**

"There's only one way to Heaven because there's only one God that exists who's made only one offer of forgiveness through His only one Son." –**Alan Shlemon**

"There is for me powerful evidence that there is something going on behind it all...It seems as though somebody has fine-tuned nature's numbers to make the universe...The impression of design is overwhelming." –**Paul Davies**

"Almost all our witnessing and Christian communication assumes that people are open to what we have to say, or at least are interested, if not in need of what we are saying. Yet most people quite simply are not open, not interested and not needy, and in much of the advanced modern world fewer people are open today than even a generation ago. Indeed, many are more hostile, and their hostility is greater than the Western church has faced for centuries…Our urgent need today is to reunite evangelism and apologetics, to make sure that our best arguments are directed toward winning people and not just winning arguments, and to seek to do all this in a manner that is true to the gospel itself." –**Os Guinness**

"The popular belief that the text of the Bible has not been accurately preserved, can be disproved by the manuscript evidence and a comparison of what the Bible says today with what the early church fathers quoted it as saying back in the earliest centuries of church history." –**Charlie Campbell**

"Wherever Jesus has been proclaimed, we see lives change for the good, nations change for the better, thieves become honest, alcoholics become sober, hateful individuals become channels of love."
–**Josh McDowell**

"It is not too much to say that it was the rise of the science of archeology that broke the deadlock between historians and the orthodox Christian. Little by little, one city after another, one civilization after another, one culture after another, whose memories were enshrined only in the Bible, were restored to their proper place in ancient history by the studies of archeologists…The over-all result is indisputable. Forgotten cities have been found, the handiwork of vanished peoples has reappeared, contemporary records of Biblical events have been unearthed and the uniqueness of biblical revelation has been emphasized by contrast and comparison to the newly understood religions of ancient peoples. Nowhere has archaeological discovery refuted the Bible as history." –**John Elder**

"The existence of the universe itself is evidence of a miracle. So when people say that they don't believe in miracles, I ask them to look around because they are living in one." –**Frank Turek**

"If you're placed in a situation where you suspect your convictions will be labeled intolerant, bigoted, narrow-minded, and judgmental, turn the tables. When someone asks for your personal views about a moral issue—homosexuality, for example—preface your remarks with a question. You say: "You know, this is actually a very personal question you're asking, and I'd be glad to answer. But before I do, I want to know if you consider yourself a tolerant person or an intolerant person. Is it safe to give my opinion, or are you going to judge me for my point of view? Do you respect diverse ideas, or do you condemn others for convictions that differ from yours?" Let them answer. If they say they're tolerant (which they probably will), then when you give your point of view it's going to be very difficult for them to call you intolerant or judgmental without looking guilty, too. This response capitalizes on the fact that there's no morally neutral ground. Everybody has a point of view they think is right and

everybody judges at some point or another. The Christian gets pigeon-holed as the judgmental one, but everyone else is judging, too. It's an inescapable consequence of believing in any kind of morality."
–**Greg Koukl**

"Remember that the Bible says "Be transformed by the renewing of your mind" not the removal of your mind." –**Andy Bannister**

"To sustain the belief that there is no God, atheism has to demonstrate infinite knowledge, which is tantamount to saying, 'I have infinite knowledge that there is no being in existence with infinite knowledge.'" –**Ravi Zacharias**

"In my experience when critics raise these objections [regarding supposed errors or contradictions in the Bible], they invariably violate one of seventeen principles for interpreting the Scriptures... For example, assuming the unexplained is unexplainable...failing to understand the context of the passage...assuming a partial report is a false report...neglecting to interpret difficult passages in light of clear ones; basing a teaching on an obscure passage; forgetting that the Bible uses nontechnical, everyday language; failing to remember the Bible uses different literary devices..." –**Norman Geisler**

"Christianity rises or falls on the resurrection of Jesus Christ from the dead. If this event is historically true, it makes all other religions false, because Jesus Christ claimed to be the one and only way to God the Father. To prove this, He predicted He would come out of the grave alive three days after He was executed. And He did."
–**Randy Alcorn**

"Many Christian college students have encountered criticisms of Christianity based on claims that early Christianity and the New Testament borrowed important beliefs and practices from a number of pagan mystery religions. Since these claims undermine such central Christian doctrines as Christ's death and resurrection, the charges are serious. But the evidence for such claims, when it even exists, often lies in sources several centuries older than the New

Testament. Moreover, the alleged parallels often result from liberal scholars uncritically describing pagan beliefs and practices in Christian language and then marveling at the striking parallels they think they've discovered." –**Ronald Nash**

"DNA is estimated to contain instructions that, if written out, would fill a thousand six-hundred-page books…The DNA is so narrow and compacted that all the genes in my body's cells would fit into an ice cube; yet if the DNA were unwound and joined together end to end, the strand could stretch from the earth to the sun and back more than four hundred times." –**Paul Brand** and **Philip Yancey**

"One of the compelling evidences God exists is the human body. Your body has 206 bones, about 700 muscles, and a heart that beats over a 100,000 times a day as it pumps about 75 gallons of blood an hour through more than 60,000 miles of veins, arteries, and capillaries. The eyes you're looking through right now are composed of more than two million working parts. Do you really believe all those muscles, bones, and organs pieced themselves together and started functioning apart from a designer?" –**Charlie Campbell**

"Frankly, a lot of cults and 'isms' also sound good at first. You cannot tell them from the real thing until about the twelfth or thirteenth lesson. Those are the lessons in which they introduce their false doctrine. Someone once said to me, 'Dr. McGee, you should not criticize so-and-so. I listened to him, and he preached the gospel.' Well, he does preach the gospel every now and then. But it is the other things he says that are in error. You see, he sows tares among the wheat."
–**J. Vernon McGee**

"Supposing there was no intelligence behind the universe, no creative mind. In that case, nobody designed my brain for the purpose of thinking. It is merely that when the atoms inside my skull happen, for physical or chemical reasons, to arrange themselves in a certain way, this gives me, as a by-product, the sensation I call thought. But, if so, how can I trust my own thinking to be true? It's like upsetting a milk jug and hoping that the way it splashes itself will give you a map of London. But if I can't trust my own thinking, of course I can't trust the arguments leading to Atheism, and therefore have no reason to be an Atheist, or anything else. Unless I believe in God, I cannot believe in thought: so I can never use thought to disbelieve in God." –**C.S. Lewis**

"Christianity is...rarely understood by those outside its bounds. In fact, this is probably one of the greatest tasks confronting the apologist—to rescue Christianity from misunderstandings."
–**Alister McGrath**

"The apostle Paul called the church "the pillar and ground of the truth" (1 Timothy 3:15). We have a duty to uphold the truth and to wield the sword of God's Word against every human speculation and every worldly hypothesis raised up against the knowledge of God."
–**John MacArthur**

"One by one the great prophets of materialism have been shown to be false prophets and have fallen aside. Marx and Freud have lost their scientific standing. Now Darwin is on the block. Some of us saw a clip of Richard Dawkins being interviewed on public television about his reaction to Michael Behe's book. You can see how insecure that man is behind his bluster, and how much he has to rely on not having Mike Behe on the program with him, or even a lesser figure like Phil Johnson. Darwinists have to rely on confining their critics in a stereotype. They have learned to keep their own philosophy on the stage with no rivals allowed, and now they have to rely almost exclusively on that cultural power." –**Phillip E. Johnson**

"While many have doubted the accuracy of the Bible, time and continued research have consistently demonstrated that the Word of God is better informed than its critics. In fact, while thousands of finds from the ancient world support in broad outline and often in detail the biblical picture, not one incontrovertible find has ever contradicted the Bible." –**Norman Geisler**

"[Richard] Dawkins insists that there is "not the smallest evidence" that atheism systematically influences people to do bad things. It's an astonishing, naive and somewhat sad statement. Dawkins is clearly an ivory tower atheist, disconnected from the real and brutal world of the twentieth century." –**Alister McGrath**

"While the new atheists complain about the evil done by religious people, the same atheists are suspiciously silent about the evil done by their fellow atheists. If we're looking at raw numbers, the impact of evil done by atheists in just a few decades of the twentieth century dwarfs anything done by theists in the last 500 years. Yet the new atheists say little about it…Over just a few decades, Stalin, Hitler, and Mao together murdered as many as 100 million people. By contrast, over a 500 year period, the Crusades, the Inquisition, and witch burnings together were responsible for about 200,000 deaths. That's far less than 1 percent of the atheist totals. (Don't get me wrong—it's still terrible. But it's nothing like the havoc imposed by unbelievers.)"
–**Frank Turek**

"We've reached the point where everybody has to preach apologetically…To be clear, I don't think such preaching is simply a matter of incorporating in every sermon arguments for the resurrection, or the existence of God, and so forth (though some of that might help). Instead, we need to actively answer objections to the gospel from inside the mindset of our cross-pressured culture on a regular basis as a part of our scriptural exposition. We need to show the consistency, coherence, and comeliness of the gospel to this generation."
–**Derek Rishmawy**

"Boldness is to be clear in the face of fear—to say what you know the word of God says even when the whole world doesn't want you to say it." –**Kevin DeYoung**

"In Jeremiah 1:9-10, God tells Jeremiah, "Behold, I have put My words in your mouth…to root out and to pull down, to destroy and to throw down, to build and to plant." To root out? To pull down? To destroy? What is God talking about? There are times for God's ambassadors when preaching the gospel is not enough. God's ambassadors are to preach the gospel and to make disciples ("to build and to plant") but sometimes before an unsaved person will embrace the gospel, we must be involved in what we might call "spiritual demolition." That is, demolishing lies and misconceptions that are keeping a person back from embracing the gospel. God wants to use us, His church, yes for the proclamation of the gospel, but also to attack error (sounds kind of strong, but notice the verse again in Jeremiah 1) with truth. He wants us to root out and pull down ideas, philosophies, and lies that keep people back from truly knowing God. This was something that Paul and Timothy did. Paul wrote, "We are destroying speculations and every lofty thing raised up against the knowledge of God" (2 Cor. 10:5). Of course, this attack on error is to be done with great humility, love and patience for the person (1 Ptr. 3:15, 2 Tim. 2:24–26)." –**Charlie Campbell**

"In private many scientists admit that science has no explanation for the beginning of life...Darwin never imagined the exquisitely profound complexity that exists even at the most basic levels of life." –**Michael Behe**

"Atheism provides a hiding place for those who do not want to acknowledge and repent of their sins." –**Dinesh D'Souza**

"The Bible—banned, burned, beloved. More widely read, more frequently attacked than any other book in history. Generations of intellectuals have attempted to discredit it; dictators of every age have outlawed it and executed those who read it. Yet soldiers carry it into battle believing it is more powerful than their weapons. Fragments of it smuggled into solitary prison cells have transformed ruthless killers into gentle saints. Pieced together scraps of Scripture have converted whole villages of pagan Indians." –**Charles Colson**

"If Jesus remained dead, how can you explain the reality of the Christian church and its phenomenal growth in the first three centuries of the Christian era? Christ's church covered the Western world by the fourth century. A religious movement built on a lie could not have accomplished that...All the power of Rome and of the religious establishment in Jerusalem was geared to stop the Christian faith. All they had to do was to dig up the grave and to present the corpse. They didn't." –**Henry Schaefer**

"I confess that when I have to argue about the truth of divine things it is a dreary task to me...while they are wanting me to argue about this point or that it seems to me like asking a man to prove that there is a sun in yonder sky. I bask in His beams, I swoon under His heat, I see by His light; and yet they ask me to prove His existence! Are the men mad? What do they want me to prove? That God hears prayer? I pray and receive answers every day. That God pardons sin? I was in my own esteem the blackest of sinners, and sunk in the depths of despair, yet I believed, and by that faith I leaped into a fullness of light and liberty at once. Why do they not try it themselves?"
–**Charles Spurgeon**

"There are only two religions, one of divine accomplishment (Christianity) and the other of human achievement (all others). Only one saves." –**Steven Lawson**

"Christians are mocked for believing in the Virgin Birth, Jesus walking on water, the Resurrection, and Jonah and the great fish. Yet those biblical miracles are nothing compared to the greatest miracle in the Bible. The greatest miracle in the Bible is not Jonah and the fish, Jesus walking on water, being born of a virgin, or even the resurrecting from the dead. The greatest miracle in the Bible is the first verse: "In the beginning God created the heavens and the earth." If that verse is true, then every other verse in the Bible is at least believable. If there is a God who created the universe out of nothing, then He can do whatever He wants that's not logically impossible inside the universe. Jonah, water walking, and resurrections are easy for that kind of Being." –**Frank Turek**

"If it were true that Christianity and science were incompatible, there would be no Christians who were respected scientists. In fact, about forty percent of professional natural scientists are practicing Christians, and many others are theists of other kinds. Fewer than thirty percent are atheists." –**Jeffrey Russell**

The rise of the cults is "directly proportional to the fluctuating emphasis which the Christian church has placed on the teaching of biblical doctrine to Christian laymen. To be sure, a few pastors, teachers, and evangelists defend adequately their beliefs, but most of them—and most of the average Christian laymen—are hard put to confront and refute a well-trained cultist of almost any variety."
–**Walter Martin**

"Just ten years ago, probably the most prominent atheist of the twentieth century, Antony Flew, concluded that a God must have designed the universe. It was shocking news and made international headlines. Flew came to believe that the extraordinarily complex genetic code in DNA simply could not be accounted for naturalistically. It didn't make logical sense to him that it had happened merely by chance, via random mutations. It is a remarkable thing that Flew had the humility and intellectual honesty to do a public about-face on all he had stood for and taught for five decades." –**Eric Metaxas**

"If the Flood were local, why did Noah have to build an Ark? He could have walked to the other side of the mountains and escaped. Traveling just 20 km per day, Noah and his family could have traveled over 3,000 km in six months. God could have simply warned Noah to flee, as He did for Lot in Sodom…If the Flood were local, why did God send the animals to the Ark to escape death? There would have been other animals to reproduce those kinds even if they had all died in the local area. Or He could have sent them to a non-flooded region. If the Flood were local, why would birds have been sent on board? These could simply have winged across to a nearby mountain range. Birds can fly several hundred kilometers in one day.…If the Flood were local, how could the waters rise to 15 cubits (8 meters) above the mountains (Gen. 7:20)? Water seeks its own level. It could not rise to cover the local mountains while leaving the rest of the world untouched." –**Ken Ham**

"A nominal Christian often discovers in suffering that his faith

has been in his church, denomination, or family tradition, but not Christ. As he faces evil and suffering, he may lose his faith. But that's actually a good thing. I have sympathy for people who lose their faith, but any faith lost in suffering wasn't a faith worth keeping."
–Randy Alcorn

"Hundreds of years before Jesus was born, prophets foretold the coming of the Messiah, or the Anointed One, who would redeem God's people. In effect, dozens of these Old Testament prophecies created a fingerprint that only the true Messiah could fit. This gave Israel a way to rule out imposters and validate the credentials of the authentic Messiah. Against astronomical odds—by one estimate, one chance in a trillion, trillion, trillion, trillion, trillion, trillion, trillion, trillion, trillion, trillion, trillion, trillion, trillion — Jesus, and only Jesus throughout history, matched this prophetic fingerprint. This confirms Jesus' identity to an incredible degree of certainty."
–Lee Strobel

"It is extremely illogical to think that Jesus Christ is a liar. Historian Philip Schaff said, 'How in the name of logic, common sense, and experience, could an imposter—that is a deceitful, selfish, depraved man—have invented, and consistently maintained from the beginning to end, the purest and noblest character known in history with the most perfect air of truth and reality? How could he have conceived and carried out a plan of unparalleled beneficence, moral magnitude, and sublimity, and sacrificed his own life for it, in the face of the strongest prejudices of his people and age?'"
–Josh McDowell

"I attack ideas. I don't attack people. And some very good people have some very bad ideas." **–Antonin Scalia**

"The book of Acts cites at least eighty–four historical facts verified by later research and archaeology. Luke's accuracy regarding details, names, and places has been acknowledged by numerous historians."
–Alex McFarland

"I submit that, far from science having buried God, not only do the results of science point toward His existence, but the scientific enterprise itself is validated by His existence. Inevitably, of course, not only those of us who do science but all of us have to choose the presuppositions with which we start. There are not many options—essentially, just two. Either human intelligence ultimately owes its origin to mindless matter or there is a Creator. It is strange that some people claim that it is their intelligence that leads them to prefer the first to the second."
–John Lennox

"A man who was merely a man and said the sort of things Jesus said would not be a great moral teacher. He would either be a lunatic—on the level with the man who says he is a poached egg—or else he would be the Devil of Hell. You must make your choice. Either this man was, and is, the Son of God: or else a madman or something worse. You can shut Him up for a fool, you can spit at Him and kill Him as a demon; or you can fall at His feet and call Him Lord and God. But let us not come with any patronizing nonsense about His being a great human teacher. He has not left that open to us. He did not intend to." **–C.S. Lewis**

"Some Bible critics argue that after Constantine accepted Christianity, the Roman Empire took control of the Bible and then "doctored" it. In other words, there was a deliberate conspiracy to change the Bible text…However, there's absolutely no evidence that the Roman Empire changed the scriptures…The problem with this theory, however, is that the Bible as we have it today can be checked against earlier copies of the scriptures [copies of the Bible that predate the time of Constantine]." **–Ed Strauss**

"Religion makes us proud of what we have done. The Gospel makes us proud of what Jesus has done." **–Tim Keller**

"If evolution happened, the fossil record should show continuous and gradual changes from the bottom to the top layers. Actually, many gaps or discontinuities appear throughout the fossil record. The fossil record has been studied so thoroughly it is safe to conclude these gaps are real; they will never be filled." –**Walter Brown**

"Atheism, I began to realize, rested on a less–than–satisfactory evidential basis. The arguments that had once seemed bold, decisive, and conclusive increasingly turned out to be circular, tentative, and uncertain." –**Alister McGrath**

"One of the most amazing facts about the early Christian belief in Jesus' resurrection was that it originated in the very city where Jesus was crucified. The Christian faith did not come to exist in some distant city, far from eyewitnesses who knew of Jesus' death and burial. No, it came into being in the very city where Jesus had been publicly crucified, under the very eyes of its enemies." –**William Craig**

"A dog barks when his master is attacked. I would be a coward if I saw that God's truth is attacked and yet would remain silent."
–**John Calvin**

"The field of apologetics deals with the hard questions posed to the Christian faith. Each of us has a worldview, whether we recognize it or not. A worldview basically offers answers to four necessary questions: origin, meaning, morality and destiny. Christian apologetics is the discipline of answering people's specific questions and making the truth claims clear. We aim to engage people in meaningful interactions with gentleness and respect, bearing in mind that behind every question is a questioner." –**Ravi Zacharias**

"The disciples had nothing to gain by lying and starting a new religion. They faced hardship, ridicule, hostility, and martyr's deaths. In light of this, they could never have sustained such unwavering motivation if they knew what they were preaching was a lie. The disciples were not fools and Paul was a cool–headed intellectual of the first rank. There would have been several opportunities over three to four decades of ministry to reconsider and renounce a lie."
–**J.P. Moreland**

"Bringing offense is one of the most potent ways you can squash your evangelistic efforts. We can be 100 percent accurate in the doctrine that we share with someone, and we can be spot-on in our description of the gospel of salvation, but if we bring offense in the process of witnessing, our listeners will likely turn away and not come back. If we truly want to be effective as missionaries on our doorsteps, we must learn to avoid being offensive when we speak." –**Ron Rhodes**

"When a Mormon says, "The Bible's inspired insofar as it has been properly translated," your first question should be, "Do you mean to say that if the Bible has been changed, it shouldn't be trusted?" They're going to say, "Of course it shouldn't be trusted if it's been changed." Then ask this question, "How many times has the Book of Mormon been changed?" The Book of Mormon has been changed hundreds of times, as a point in fact. This is very well documented. We do have the original documents of the Book of Mormon and we have the current ones and there are hundreds of changes. So even by their own rule, the Book of Mormon is a fraud." –**Greg Koukl**

"Many people entertain the idea that Christianity, like almost any other religion, is basically a system of beliefs—you know, a set of doctrines or a code of behavior, a philosophy, an ideology. But that's a myth. Christianity is not at all like Buddhism or Islam or Confucianism. The founders of those religions said (in effect), 'Here is what I teach. Believe my teachings. Follow my philosophy.' Jesus said, 'Follow me' (Matthew 9:9). Leaders of the world's religions said, 'What do you think about what I teach?' Jesus said, 'Who do you say I am?' (Luke 9:20)." –**Josh McDowell**

"God's Word has stood against its critics for hundreds of years. They come, they criticize, they disagree among themselves and they disappear—leaving only a paper trail of unbelief as their legacy. But for those who believe the Bible to be without error, and who believe it is God's clear revelation for modern man, it consistently proves to be a reliable guide to the way of salvation and for every aspect of the Christian life." –**Brian Edwards**

"Is it really credible that random processes could have constructed a reality...which excels in every sense anything produced by the intelligence of man?" –**Michael Denton**

"No one statement wrested from its context is a sufficient warrant for actions that plainly controvert other commands. How excellent a thing it would be if the whole Church of Christ had learned that no law of life may be based upon an isolated text. Every false teacher who has divided the Church, has had, "it is written" on which to hang his doctrine." –**G. Campbell Morgan**

"There are dozens of ancient texts in the records of the Assyrians, Babylonians, and Romans that verify details in the Bible. As far as persons are concerned, external sources verify that more than 50 persons mentioned in the Old Testament and 30 persons written about in the New Testament were actual historical figures. Think of that! More than 80 persons in the Bible are talked about in historical sources outside the Bible! We are not reading about mythological characters when we read the Bible. We're reading about real people."
–**Charlie Campbell**

"I heard the story of a man, a blasphemer...an atheist, who was converted singularly by a sinful action of his. He had written on a piece of paper, "God is nowhere," and ordered his child to read it, for he would make him an atheist too. The child spelled it, "God is n–o–w h–e–r–e. God is now here." It was a truth instead of a lie, and the arrow pierced the man's own heart." –**Charles Spurgeon**

"Sometimes when I listen to people who say they have lost their faith, I am far less surprised than they expect. If their view of God is what they say, then it is only surprising that they did not reject it much earlier. Other people have a concept of God so fundamentally false that it would be better for them to doubt than to remain devout. The more devout they are, the uglier their faith will become since it is based on a lie. Doubt in such a case is not only highly understandable, it is even a mark of spiritual and intellectual sensitivity to error, for their picture is not of God but an idol." –**Os Guinness**

"It's ironic that Isaac Newton, discoverer of the laws of motion that were later used by others to attempt to contradict parts of the Bible, was one of its greatest defenders. He wrote several papers supporting the accuracy of the text and spoke out against the Biblical critics of his day." –**Ralph Muncaster**

"I have a fundamental belief in the Bible as the Word of God, written by those who were inspired. I study the Bible daily." –**Isaac Newton**

"Bertrand Russell (1872–1970) argued that if everything needs a cause, then so does God. And if all things do not need a cause, then neither does the world. But in neither case do we need a First Cause. The major premise is false. Theists do not claim that everything needs a cause. The principle of causality states only that everything that begins (or is finite) needs a cause. If something does not have a beginning, then it obviously does not need a Beginner. Nontheists such as Russell acknowledge that the universe does not need a cause—it is just "there." If the universe can just "be there" without a cause, why can't God?" –**Norman Geisler**

"From chilling headlines and disgusted tweets to deep wounds and sobbing tears, we all know it: Moral relativism is a myth. There's right and wrong and it's imprinted on our souls." –**Matt Smethurst**

"False teachers invite people to come to the Master's table because of what's on it, not because they love the Master." –**Hank Hanegraaff**

"We are called to be the people of the truth, even when the truth is not popular and even when the truth is denied by the culture around us. Christians have found themselves in this position before, and we will again. God's truth has not changed. The holy Scriptures have not changed. The gospel of Jesus Christ has not changed. The church's mission has not changed. Jesus Christ is the same, yesterday, today and tomorrow." –**Albert Mohler**

"God exists whether or not men may choose to believe in Him. The reason why many people do not believe in God is not so much that it is intellectually impossible to believe in God, but because belief in God forces that thoughtful person to face the fact that he is accountable to such a God." –**Robert Laidlaw**

"All I am in private life is a literary critic and historian, that's my job... And I'm prepared to say on that basis if anyone thinks the Gospels are either legends or novels, then that person is simply showing his incompetence as a literary critic. I've read a great many novels and I know a fair amount about the legends that grew up among early people, and I know perfectly well the Gospels are not that kind of stuff." –**C.S. Lewis**

"Whatever you currently believe about Jesus of Nazareth, you owe it to yourself to investigate Him thoroughly. It makes little sense to ignore the one solitary life that continues to impact you in eternity if His claims are true." –**Frank Turek**

"The Bible is unmistakably the most unique book ever written. For instance, it was written by 40 authors over a span of roughly 1,500-years in diverse places, times, and languages. It has unique teachings that include the Trinity and salvation by grace (for example, Ephesians 2:8–9). And the Bible has had more impact on individual people, governments, and civilizations than any book ever written. The historical and cultural impact of the Bible is simply unparalleled. And what's most amazing is that even among these various factors, the Bible has an overarching focus on Jesus Christ and his offer of salvation." –**Josh McDowell**

"If you deny the existence of God, any moral values you advocate for are nothing more than your personal preferences." –**Andy Bannister**

"Now if the religious skeptic is right, we can know nothing about God. And if we can know nothing about God, how can we know God so well that we can know that he cannot be known? How can we know that God cannot and did not reveal himself—and perhaps even through human reason?" –**Peter Kreeft** and **Ronald Tacelli**

"The Bible's historical accuracy is a reminder that while "the heavens declare the glory of God," there's also plenty of evidence among the rubble and ruins." –**Charles Colson**

"The empire of Caesar is gone; the legions of Rome are smouldering in the dust…the prince of the pharoahs is fallen; the pyramids they raised to be their tombs are sinking every day in the desert sands… but the Word of God still survives: All things that threatened to extinguish it have only aided it; and it proves every day how transient is the noblest monument that men can build, how enduring is the least Word that God has spoken." –**Albert Cummins**

"God put enough into the world to make faith in Him a reasonable thing, but He left enough out to make it impossible to live by reason alone." –**Ravi Zacharias**

"Science itself is steadily nailing the lid on atheism's coffin."
–**Lee Strobel**

"An average healthy human brain contains some 200 billion nerve cells connected to one another through hundreds of trillions of synapses…The study's results showed a single human brain has more information processing units than all the computers, routers, and Internet connections on Earth…The equivalent man–made devices would require at least 10 mega–watts of power to operate. The human brain uses only about 10 watts."
–**Jeffrey Tomkins** and **Randy Guliuzza**

"It's scientifically inaccurate to say a human fetus isn't a person simply because he's at an earlier stage of development than an infant. A toddler isn't less human because he's not yet an adolescent. Likewise, an unborn child isn't less human than a 6–month–old."
–**Randy Alcorn**

"I was brought up to believe that the Bible was the Word of God. In early life I accepted it as such upon the authority of my parents, and never gave the question any serious thought. But later in life my faith in the Bible was utterly shattered through the influence of the writings of a very celebrated, scholarly and brilliant skeptic. I found myself face to face with the question, Why do you believe the Bible is the Word of God? I had no satisfactory answer. I determined to go to the bottom of this question. If satisfactory proof could not be found that the Bible was God's Word I would give the whole thing up, cost what it might. If satisfactory proof could be found that the Bible was God's Word I would take my stand upon it, cost what it might. I doubtless had many friends who could have answered the question satisfactorily, but I was unwilling to confide to them the struggle that was going on in my own heart; so I sought help from God and from books, and after much painful study and thought came out of the darkness of skepticism into the broad daylight of faith and certainty that the Bible from beginning to end is God's Word." –**R.A. Torrey**

"Most atheists, in my experience, have no good reasons for their disbelief. Rather they've learned to simply repeat the slogan, "There's no good evidence for God's existence!" In the case of a Christian who has no good reasons for what he believes, this slogan serves as an effective conversation–stopper. But if we have good reasons for our beliefs, then this slogan serves rather as a conversation–starter."
–**William Craig**

"Perhaps the greatest difference between the Bible and all other religious books is that the Bible teaches a message of salvation by grace, whereas every other religious system teaches salvation by human works." –**Nathan Busenitz**

"Is the Bible the Word of God? Then let us all resolve from this day forward to prize the Bible more. Let us not fear being idolaters of this blessed book. Men may easily make an idol of the Church, of ministers, of sacraments, or of intellect. Men cannot make an idol of the Word. Let us regard all who would damage the authority of the Bible, or impugn its credit, as spiritual robbers. We are traveling through a wilderness: they rob us of our only guide. We are voyaging over a stormy sea: they rob us of our only compass. We are toiling over a weary road: they pluck our staff out of our hands. And what do these spiritual robbers give us in place of the Bible? What do they offer as a safer guide and better provision for our souls? Nothing! Absolutely nothing! Big swelling words! Empty promises of new light! High sounding jargon; but nothing substantial and real! They would fain take from us the bread of life, and they do not give us in its place so much as a stone. Let us turn a deaf ear to them. Let us firmly grasp and prize the Bible more and more, the more it is assaulted...God has given us the Bible to be a light to guide us to everlasting life. Let us not neglect this precious gift. Let us read it diligently, walk in its light, and we shall be saved." –**J.C. Ryle**

"As Christians we accept one big miracle: God, and everything else makes sense. An atheist denies God and has to have a miracle for every other thing." –**John MacArthur**

"Another misconception about the Bible is that it was merely created by a select few in order to consolidate, gain or maintain power and prestige. Given the adversity faced by the Hebrew people and, later, the persecution suffered by Christians, this explanation is far from plausible. For instance, rather than gaining power or prestige, the early Christians were severely oppressed, while many others were killed—martyred for believing the message of the gospel."
–**Robert Velarde**

"Why would the apostles lie [about the resurrection]?...Liars always lie for selfish reasons. If they lied, what was their motive, what did they get out of it? What they got out of it was misunderstanding, rejection, persecution, torture, and martyrdom. Hardly a list of perks!"
–**Peter Kreeft**

"The general public doesn't often recognize that operation science—the science that most often brings us technological advances—is not the same as origin or historical science. Therefore, when atheistic scientists speak on matters of history, the public tends to believe them due to the prestige of "science." Unfortunately, the "scientific" conclusions offered are often materialistic philosophy flown under the banner of science." –**Frank Turek**

"When a woman decides to kill her child, that decision infringes on a child's right to life, liberty and the pursuit of happiness. Abortion says the rights of stronger and louder women trump the rights of those who can not speak." –**Devin Sena**

"God knows in advance who will accept the message of the gospel, and He is not limited in how He can bring the gospel to them. The normative way should be through preaching (Matthew 28:18-20; Romans 10:14-17), but one can be saved through reading the Bible (Psalm 119:130; Hebrews 4:12). If necessary, God can get the message to one through angels (Revelation 14:6), or through visions (Daniel 4:5, 35), or through dreams (Daniel 2, 7). God also can speak from heaven through an audible voice (Acts 9) or through an inner voice in the heart as He did to the prophets (e.g., Hosea 1:1)."
–**Norman Geisler**

"Nonsense remains nonsense, even when talked by world-famous scientists." –**John Lennox**

"Some say Christianity is just a crutch. But let's turn the question on its edge for a moment. Is atheism an emotional crutch, wishful thinking? The ax cuts both ways. Perhaps atheists are rejecting God because they've had a bad relationship with their father. Instead of inventing God, have atheists invented non-God? Have they invented atheism to escape some of the frightening implications of God's existence? Think about it." –**Greg Koukl**

"There is more than sufficient evidence to establish the fact that the Old Testament we have today is an accurate copy of the original. The Jewish men who copied the scriptures knew exactly how many letters were in every line of every book and how many times each word occurred in each book. This enabled them to check for errors. The first-century Roman historian Flavius Josephus, who was also a Jew, stated: 'We have given practical proof of our reverence for our own Scriptures. For although such long ages have now passed, no one has ventured either to add, or to remove, or to alter a syllable; and it is an instinct with every Jew, from the day of his birth, to regard them as the decrees of God, to abide by them, and, if need be, cheerfully to die for them.'" –**Charlie Campbell**

"Do we have an accurate copy of the original New Testament? We do. By comparing the thousands of handwritten Greek manuscripts and quotations from the ancient world, scholars can reconstruct the text of the New Testament documents with more than 99 percent accuracy. And the less than one percent in question affects no doctrine of the Christian faith." –**Frank Turek**

"Voltaire is reported to have said that within 100 years of his day the Bible would be a forgotten book. In a strange twist of irony, within a century of his death, one of his homes in France would belong to the Geneva Bible Society and serve as the place where Bibles were printed and distributed." –**Ravi Zacharias**

"One of the reasons I started taking this anti-evolutionary view, or let's call it non-evolutionary view, was last year I had a sudden realization that for over twenty years I had thought I was working on evolution in some way. One morning I woke up and something had happened in the night and it struck me that I had been working on this stuff for twenty years and there was not one thing I knew about it. That's quite a shock to learn that one can be misled so long...For the last few weeks I've tried putting a simple question to various people and groups of people. The question is this: Can you tell me anything you know about evolution, any one thing, any one thing that you think is true? I tried that question on the geology staff at the Field Museum of Natural History and the only answer I got was silence. I tried it on the members of the Evolutionary Morphology Seminar at the University of Chicago, a very prestigious body of evolutionists, and all I got there was silence for a long time and eventually one person said, "I do know one thing—it ought not to be taught in high school."...The level of knowledge about evolution is remarkably shallow. We know it ought not to be taught in the high school and that's all we know about it." –**Colin Patterson**

"The fact is, there is virtually no support for evolution in the fossil

record. There is no actual fossil evidence that shows primitive life forms evolved into complex life forms because no credible transitional fossils between any groups of animals have been found. Honest paleontologists admit this. The late Dr. Colin Patterson, former senior paleontologist at the British Museum of Natural History and editor of its journal, was asked why he didn't include photographs of transitional fossils in his book, *Evolution*. He replied, "If I knew of any, fossils or living, I would certainly have included them."
–Dan Story

"Do not become discouraged if you do not see an immediate conversion after your dialogue... Just focus on respectfully telling the truth and faithfully planting and/or watering the seed of the gospel. It is then in God's sovereign hands. As the Christian singer Keith Green once said, 'Do your best, pray that it's blessed, and the Lord will take care of the rest.'" **–Ron Rhodes**

"The New Testament books did not become authoritative for the Church because they were formally included in a canonical list; on the contrary, the Church included them in her canon because she already regarded them as divinely inspired." **–F.F. Bruce**

"Another indication that the Flood was indeed a world–encompassing catastrophe is the existence of 250–300 accounts of the flood all around the world. These stories are found among the most remote tribes in China, India, the mountains of the Himalayas, Scandinavia, Peru, and North America, and even among the indigenous peoples of Hawaii, New Zealand, and the Polynesian archipelago. It is not by chance that all these stories are similar; they all tell about the same event...The evolution theory has no good explanation for the existence of all these tales of a Flood. Because, according to that theory, humans spread around the world from prehistoric times and the various peoples did not have any contact with one another in their earliest history. So they could never have adopted stories from one another..." **–Ben Hobrink**

"My father's life was changed right before my eyes [when he trusted Christ]. It was like someone reached down and switched on a light inside him. He touched alcohol only once after that. He got the drink only as far as his lips and that was it—after forty years of drinking! He didn't need it any more. Fourteen months later, he died from complications of his alcoholism. But in that fourteen-month period over a hundred people in the area around my tiny hometown committed their lives to Jesus Christ because of the change they saw in the town drunk, my dad." –**Josh McDowell**

"Everyone worships—even an atheist. He worships himself. When men reject God they worship false gods. That, of course, is what God forbids in the first commandment." –**John MacArthur**

"Why do bad things happen to good people? The Christian answer is that there are no good people. None of us deserves the life that we have, which is a gratuitous gift from God." –**Dinesh D'Souza**

"Just one living cell in the human body is, more complex than New York City." –**Linus Pauling**

"It was my science that drove me to the conclusion that the world is much more complicated than can be explained by science, it is only through the supernatural that I can understand the mystery of existence." –**Allan Sandage**

"God never performed a miracle to convince an atheist, because His ordinary works can provide sufficient evidence." –**Ariel Roth**

"I think [Andy] Stanley is only half right when he says, "Appealing to post-Christian people on the basis of the authority of Scripture has essentially the same effect as a Muslim imam appealing to you on the basis of the authority of the Quran." He is right in that this happens. God's inspired word is sometimes heard with no effect. But not always, and not usually. It is different from the Quran. It is God-breathed (2 Timothy 3:16). It is not preached in vain—especially not when, in the hands of a Spirit-filled preacher, the truth and beauty of its depths and heights are spoken with clarity and conviction for what they really are." –**John Piper**

"I believe it takes far more faith to be an atheist than to believe in God. Atheists believe that everything that exists (the entire universe with its billions of stars and planets) came from nothing and by nothing. Nobody x Nothing = Everything. That takes a lot of faith!" –**Charlie Campbell**

"Christianity today is in conflict; in conflict against the secular world; in conflict with world religions—which are hostile to us—in conflict against the Kingdom of the Cults—and the Occult; in conflict against corrupt theology in our theological seminaries—and oftentimes in our pulpits; in conflict against all forms of evil surrounding us on all sides. And it is a foolish person indeed, who does not recognize that the Church was born in conflict; lives in conflict, and will triumph in conflict. We have been called to be soldiers of the cross. And if we're going to be soldiers of the cross that means that we have to be attired to fight. That's why Paul could say here in 2 Timothy, chapter 4 — I have fought the good fight [v. 7]. He did not say, "I have taken the long vacation." I have fought the good fight, I finished the course, I kept the faith. But the problem we are facing today in Christianity—and one of the reasons why we are in crisis—is this: A large section of the Christian Church simply will not come into conflict with the world. And that, is one of our greatest drawbacks." –**Walter Martin**

"If your creed and Scripture do not agree, cut your creed to pieces, but make it agree with this book. If there be anything in the church to which you belong which is contrary to the inspired Word, leave that church." –**Charles Spurgeon**

"According to some of the church fathers, the supernatural darkness that accompanied the crucifixion was noticed throughout the world at the time. Tertullian mentioned this event in his Apologeticum, a defense of Christianity written to pagan skeptics: "At the moment of Christ's death, the light departed from the sun, and the land was darkened at noonday, which wonder is related in your own annals and is preserved in your archives to this day." –**John MacArthur**

"When someone says to me, "Reincarnation was originally part of Christian teaching, but was taken out of the Bible in the fourth century," I always ask them to explain how that works…How does someone remove select lines of text from tens of thousands of handwritten documents that had been circulating around the Mediterranean region for over three hundred years? This would be like trying to secretly remove a paragraph from all the copies of yesterday's L.A. Times. It can't be done." –**Greg Koukl**

"Why would a bacteria be considered life on Mars and a heartbeat not considered life on Earth?" –**Unknown**

"Atheistic evolutionists believe that nothing created everything—a scientific impossibility. It could not happen. So they redefine the word 'nothing' to mean 'something,' so that in their unthinking minds, they can justify their foolishness." –**Ray Comfort**

"To be ignorant and simple now—not to be able to meet the enemies on their own ground—would be to throw down our weapons and to betray our uneducated brethren who have, under God, no defense but us against the intellectual attacks of the heathen. Good philosophy must exist, if for no other reason, because bad philosophy needs to be answered." –**C.S. Lewis**

"For the scientist who has lived by his faith in the power of reason, the story ends like a bad dream. He has scaled the mountains of ignorance; he is about to conquer the highest peak; as he pulls himself over the final rock, he is greeted by a band of theologians who have been sitting there for centuries." –**Robert Jastrow**

"It is generally the man who is not ready to argue, who is ready to sneer." –**G.K. Chesterton**

"To talk of comparing the Bible with other "sacred books" so called, such as the Koran…or the book of Mormon, is positively absurd. You might as well compare the sun with a rushlight, or Skiddaw with a molehill, or St. Paul's with an Irish hovel, or the Portland vase with a garden pot, or the Kohinoor diamond with a bit of glass. God seems to have allowed the existence of these pretended revelations, in order to prove the immeasurable superiority of His own Word." –**J.C. Ryle**

"In 56 A.D. [the apostle] Paul wrote that over 500 people had seen the risen Jesus and that most of them were still alive (1 Corinthians 15:6ff.). It passes the bounds of credibility that the early Christians could have manufactured such a tale and then preached it among those who might easily have refuted it simply by producing the body of Jesus." –**John Warwick Montgomery**

"As if they had minds of their own, your new cells—some of them eventually reproducing in the womb at a rate of more than 100,000 per second—knew where to go and what to do in order to become each of your major organs. How did certain cells "know" to become heart cells, while others "knew" to become brain cells? There is no known material explanation for their goal-directedness."
–**Frank Turek**

"The Holy Spirit sets His seal in the soul of every believer to the Divine authority of the Bible. It is possible to get to a place where we need no argument to prove that the Bible is God's Word. Christ says, "My sheep know my voice," and God's children know His voice, and I know that the voice that speaks to me from the pages of that Book is the voice of my Father. You will sometimes meet a pious old lady, who tells you that she knows that the Bible is God's Word, and when you ask her for a reason for believing that it is God's Word she can give you none, She simply says: "I know it is God's Word." You say: "That is mere superstition." Not at all. She is one of Christ's sheep, and recognizes her Shepherd's voice from every other voice. She is one of God's children, and knows the voice which speaks to her from the Bible is the voice of God." –**R.A. Torrey**

"Evolutionary biologists have been able to pretend to know how complex biological systems originated only because they treated them as black boxes. Now that biochemists have opened the black boxes and seen what is inside, they know the Darwinian theory is just a story, not a scientific explanation." –**Phillip E. Johnson**

"Be very sure of this—people never reject the Bible because they cannot understand it. They understand it only too well; they understand that it condemns their own behavior; they understand that it witnesses against their own sins, and summons them to judgment."
–**J.C. Ryle**

"Not one piece of evidence has ever been found to support the Book of Mormon—not a trace of the large cities it names, no ruins, no coins, no letters or documents or monuments, nothing in writing. Not even one of the rivers or mountains or any of the topography it mentions has ever been identified." –**Dave Hunt**

"One key and defining attribute of God that does not appear in any other world religion or system is the biblical use of the term "Father." Over 70 times in the New Testament alone, God is described as "Father" to His children. No major world religion describes the relationship between its creator and its adherents in terms of a father." –**Ergun Caner**

"The existence of biological information in DNA also points toward a Creator. Each of our cells contains the precise assembly instructions for every protein out of which our bodies are made, all spelled out in a four-letter chemical alphabet. Nature can produce patterns, but whenever we see information—whether it's in a book or a computer program—we know there's intelligence behind it." –**Lee Strobel**

"The Quran, like other ancient religious writings, has made some serious errors when it comes to science—errors that prove it cannot be the product of an omniscient, divine mind...the Quran speaks of a man traveling until he actually finds the place the Sun descends down into the Earth. It says he traveled "till, when he reached the setting-place of the Sun, he found it setting in a muddy spring" (18:86). This is an error of astronomical proportions...But, you could get away with a statement like that in certain parts of the world in the seventh century...Other scientific errors in the Quran include a hard sky that can fall on the inhabitants of the Earth, stars that fly away when Abraham glances at them, a moon that is further away than the stars, mountains that were created to hold down the earth and prevent earthquakes, and meteors that are a form of divine retribution being hurled at devils who might try to spy on the heavenly council."–**Charlie Campbell**

"The Christian faith does not call for us to put our minds on the shelf, to fly in the face of common sense and history, or to make a leap of faith into the dark. The rational person, fully apprised of the evidence, can confidently believe." –**William Craig**

"God doesn't normally allow innocent people to suffer or die. He's only done that once: it was with His Son Jesus." –**Alan Shlemon**

"Supposing you eliminated suffering, what a dreadful place the world would be! I would almost rather eliminate happiness. The world would be the most ghastly place because everything that corrects the tendency of this unspeakable little creature, man, to feel over-important and over-pleased with himself would disappear. He's bad enough now, but he would be absolutely intolerable if he never suffered." –**Malcolm Muggeridge**

"Those who expected the [Dead Sea] Scrolls to produce a radical revision of the Bible have been disappointed, for these texts have only verified the reliability and stability of the Old Testament as it appears in our modern translations." –**Randall Price**

"The Bible towers in content above all earlier religious literature; and it towers just as impressively over all subsequent literature in the direct simplicity of its message and…its appeal to men of all lands and times." –**W.F. Albright**

"I said, "Can I ask you a question? On every university campus I visit, somebody stands up and says that God is an evil God to allow all this evil into our world. This person typically says, 'A plane crashes: Thirty people die, and twenty people live. What kind of a God would arbitrarily choose some to live and some to die?'" I continued, "but when we play God and determine whether a child within a mother's womb should live, we argue for that as a moral right. So when human beings are given the privilege of playing God, it's called a moral right. When God plays God, we call it an immoral act. Can you justify this for me?" That was the end of the conversation." –**Ravi Zacharias**

"The men who penned the Scriptures revealed several amazing facts about the Earth and the universe thousands of years before scientists discovered these declarations to be true. This is astounding!...These men lived two, three, four thousand years before the invention of the telescope, microscopes, satellites, deep–diving submarines, and other technologies were around...So how did they know these things? They had "inside information" from the One who created the universe." –**Charlie Campbell**

"Scientists of Darwin's day saw the cell as little more than a simple blob of protoplasm. They thought natural laws could perhaps create such a cell. But the science of today shows that the cell is a world of astonishing complexity containing all sorts of microscopic machinery and thousands of pages of genetic programming. If atheists could offer a naturalistic explanation for this, they would. Instead, they can do little more than belch insults or offer unsupported speculations that, even if true, do nothing to solve the problem." –**Frank Turek**

"Sometimes God permits evil by giving people over to their sins (see Romans 1:24–32), and this itself leads to the deterioration and ultimate death of an evil culture, which is a mercy to surrounding cultures. The most morally corrupt ancient cultures no longer exist." –**Randy Alcorn**

Contrary to what some critics of the Bible say, Jesus had a high view of women. "He invites Mary to join a theological discussion when her sister wants her in the kitchen to help make dinner. He banters respectfully with the Samaritan women at the well, whom most Jews would have shunned. He heals sick women. He rescues, from stoning, a girl accused of adultery. When a female "sinner" crashes a

dinner party, He treats her with more respect than His host."
–**David Marshall**

"Hundreds of specific prophecies have been fulfilled, often long after the prophetic writer had passed away. For example, the prophet Daniel predicted around 538 BC in Daniel 9:24–27 that Christ would come as Israel's promised Savior and prince 483 years after the Persian emperor would give the Jews authority to rebuild Jerusalem. At the time of the prophecy, Jerusalem was in ruins. Yet this was clearly fulfilled hundreds of years later in Jesus." –**Alex McFarland**

"Skeptics are caught in a dilemma. If they say history cannot be known, then they lose the ability to say evolution is true and Christianity is false. If they admit history can be known, then they must deal with the multiple lines of historical evidence for creation and Christianity." –**Norman Geisler**

"The simple record of these three short years of [Jesus's] active life has done more to regenerate and soften mankind than all the discourses of philosophers and all the exhortations of moralists."
–**William Lecky**

"The indisputable fact is that all the religions of the world put together have in three thousand years not managed to kill anywhere near the number of people killed in the name of atheism in the past few decades. It's time to abandon the mindlessly repeated mantra that religious belief has been the main source of human conflict and violence. Atheism, not religion, is responsible for the worst mass murders in history" –**Dinesh D'Souza**

"In the Gospels we see Jesus reference Abel, Noah, Abraham, Sodom and Gomorrah, Isaac and Jacob, manna in the wilderness, the serpent in the wilderness, Moses as the lawgiver, David and Solomon, the Queen of Sheba, Elijah and Elisha, the widow of Zerephath, Naaman, Zechariah, and even Jonah, never questioning a single event, a single miracle, or a single historical claim. Jesus clearly believed in the historicity of biblical history." –**Kevin DeYoung**

"The extreme rarity of transitional forms in the fossil record persists as the trade secret of paleontology. The evolutionary trees that adorn our textbooks have data only at the tips and nodes of their branches; the rest is inference, however reasonable, not the evidence of fossils."
–Stephen Jay Gould

"But many children suffer; why doesn't God protect them?" We don't know the answer, but we also don't know how often God does protect children. The concept of guardian angels seems to be suggested by various passages (see, for example, Matthew 18:10). God gives us a brief, dramatic look into the unseen world in which righteous angels battle evil ones, intervening on behalf of God's people (see Daniel 10:12–13, 20). How many angels has God sent to preserve the lives of children and shield them from harm? My earliest memory is of falling into deep water and nearly drowning; someone my family didn't know rescued me. As a parent and a grandparent, I have seen many "close calls" where it appears a child should have died or suffered a terrible injury, but somehow escaped both. This thought, of course, doesn't keep a parent's heart from breaking when her child suffers or dies. Still, though I can't prove it, I'm convinced God prevents far more evil than he allows." **–Randy Alcorn**

"Some atheists are trying to pull down anything that reminds people of God. But they will never pull down the stars." **–Charlie Campbell**

"At this time there was a wise man who was called Jesus. And his conduct was good, and he was known to be virtuous. And many people from among the Jews and the other nations became his disciples. Pilate condemned Him to be crucified to die. And those who had become his disciples did not abandon his discipleship. They reported that He had appeared to them three days after his crucifixion and that He was alive." **–Flavius Josephus**

"There is a virtual consensus among scholars who study Jesus' resurrection that, subsequent to Jesus' death by crucifixion, his disciples really believed that he appeared to them risen from the dead. This conclusion has been reached by data that suggest that (1) the

disciples themselves claimed that the risen Jesus had appeared to them, and (2) subsequent to Jesus' death by crucifixion, his disciples were radically transformed from fearful, cowering individuals who denied and abandoned him at his arrest and execution into bold proclaimers of the gospel of the risen Lord. They remained steadfast in the face of imprisonment, torture, and martyrdom. It is very clear that they sincerely believed that Jesus rose from the dead."
–**Gary Habermas**

"One is faced with the fact that the only place one can prove absolutely that God is a God of love and grace is from Scripture. If one accepts the doctrine of God's love and grace as revealed in the Bible, how can that person question, then, that the same Bible teaches eternal punishment?" –**John Walvoord**

"Sometimes detractors to Christianity object to the idea of God's existence because of the occurrence of "evil" natural disasters like earthquakes and floods, etc. God created a natural world that is good in that it accomplishes certain things. In order for plants to grow and to continue to nourish humans, the crust of the earth must be replenished. Plate tectonics is one thing that accomplishes this. The incidental by-products are things like earthquakes. It is because there is an ecosystem that God made in the physical universe that has necessary contingencies, and sometimes people get in the way of those things and get killed. That is tragic, but it doesn't mean that the earthquake itself is immoral. It is only tragic because it destroys human beings who have value. If human beings didn't have value, there would be no tragedy. The real question for the atheist is, "Where do human beings derive transcendent value?" The value comes from the God who created them in His image." –**Greg Koukl**

"There's more code and sophisticated nanomachinery in just one of your forty trillion cells than in your smartphone and probably every other gadget you own. If the code and nanomachinery in your smartphone requires intelligence, wouldn't the far superior technology inside of you also require intelligence?" –**Frank Turek**

"Fictional gods may well be enemies of reason: the God of the Bible certainly is not. The very first of the biblical Ten Commandments contains the instruction to 'love the Lord your God with all your mind'. This should be enough to tell us that God is not to be regarded as an enemy of reason. After all, as Creator he is responsible for the very existence of the human mind." **–John Lennox**

"Another problem in the theory of evolution is that nearly all groups of animals appear suddenly and simultaneously in the strata of the earth. And not in primitive forms, but fully developed. According to the theory of evolution, this was just under 600 million years ago. It is certainly not the case, as most school textbooks would have us believe, that the various groups came into being consecutively and very gradually. According to the doctrine of evolution, no life occurred in 4 billion years from the beginning of the earth, with the exception of a few single-celled organisms. But suddenly we find in strata of 600 million years old representatives of all the larger groups in the animal kingdom, except the insects and vertebrates. Prominent evolutionists write, "Within just a few million years, nearly every major kind of animal anatomy appears in the fossil record for the first time." **–Ben Hobrink**

"Atheism is so senseless. When I look at the solar system. I see the earth at the right distance from the sun to receive the proper amounts of heat and light. This did not happen by chance." **–Isaac Newton**

"The evidence for the resurrection is better than for claimed miracles in any other religion. It's outstandingly different in quality and quantity." **–Antony Flew**

"In Acts 17:26, in the midst of an evangelistic lecture to secular, pagan philosophers, Paul makes the case that God created all the races "from one man." Paul's Greek listeners saw other races as barbarian, but against such views of racial superiority Paul makes the case that all races have the same Creator and are of one stock. Since all are made in God's image, every human life is of infinite and equal value (Gen. 9:5–6)." **–Tim Keller**

"Many who've never taken the time to seriously study the Bible think the Bible is a dusty old outdated book that has been disproved by scientific discoveries, when actually several details in the Bible have been *confirmed* by scientific discoveries." –**Charlie Campbell**

"Richard Dawkins admits that the amount of information in a one-celled life (like an amoeba) has as much information in its DNA as 1,000 *Encyclopaedia Britannicas*! Now, believing that 1,000 encyclopedias came into existence without any intelligent intervention is like believing that an entire bookstore resulted from an explosion in a printing shop. I don't have enough faith to believe that!"
–**Frank Turek**

"To suppose that the eye, with all its inimitable [matchless] contrivances [plans] for adjusting the focus to different distances, for admitting different amounts of light, and for the correction of spherical and chromatic aberration, could have been formed by natural selection, seems, I freely confess, absurd in the highest possible degree."
–**Charles Darwin**

"God maintains a delicate balance between keeping his existence sufficiently evident so people will know He's there and yet hiding his presence enough so that people who want to choose to ignore Him can do it. This way, their choice of destiny is really free."
–**J.P. Moreland**

"When we give our kids direction and ask them to accept this direction as a reflection of their love for us, we must step away and give them the freedom to respond (or rebel) freely. If we are "ever-present", their response will be coerced; they will behave in a particular way not because they love us, but because they know we are present (and they fear the consequence of rebellion). If God exists, it is reasonable that He would remain hidden (to some degree) to allow us the freedom to respond from a position of love, rather than fear."
–**J. Warner Wallace**

"We often read that Islam is the fastest-growing religion. Not true.

Christianity is the fastest-growing religion in the world today. Islam is second. While Islam grows mainly through reproduction—which is to say by Muslims having large families—Christianity spreads through rapid conversion as well as natural increase."
–Dinesh D'Souza

"Other religious leaders say, "Follow me and I'll show you how to find the truth." But Jesus says, "I am the truth." Other religious leaders say, "Follow me and I'll show you the way to salvation." But Jesus says, "I am the way to eternal life." Other religious leaders say, "Follow me and I'll show you how you can become enlightened." But Jesus said, "I am the light of the world." See the difference? There are drastic and irreconcilable differences between Christianity and all other belief systems." **–Lee Strobel**

"The evidence for our New Testament writings is ever so much greater than the evidence for many writings of classical authors, the authenticity of which no one dreams of questioning. And if the New Testament were a collection of secular writings, their authenticity would generally be regarded as beyond all doubt." **–F.F. Bruce**

"The positive evidence for Darwinism is confined to small-scale evolutionary changes like insects developing insecticide resistance...Evidence like that for insecticide resistance confirms the Darwinian selection mechanism for small-scale changes, but hardly warrants the grand extrapolation that Darwinists want. It is a huge leap going from insects developing insecticide resistance via the Darwinian mechanism of natural selection and random variation to the very emergence of insects in the first place by that same mechanism."
–William Dembski

"If you are concerned about your loved ones that won't be in Heaven, the most irrational thing you could do if you are truly concerned about those on the outside is to remain outside yourself."
–C.S. Lewis

"Controversy is never a very happy thing for the child of God—he would rather be in communion with his Lord than be engaged in defending the faith or in attacking error. But the soldier of Christ must follow his Master's commands." –**Charles Spurgeon**

"We have no acceptable theory of evolution at the present time. There is none; and I cannot accept the theory that I teach to my students each year. Let me explain. I teach the synthetic theory known as the neo-Darwinian one, for one reason only; not because it's good, we know that it is bad, but because there isn't any other. Whilst waiting to find something better you are taught something which is known to be inexact." –**Jerome Lejeune**

"Indifference, timidity, compromise, and nonresistance are all ruled out as options for Christians when the gospel is under attack."
–**John MacArthur**

"Part of the miracle of the resurrection is that it so empowered a ragtag band of fishermen and tax collectors that they were emboldened to stand against all earthly authority and power, and ultimately would upend the once inviolable order of the mighty Roman Empire. History tells us that this happened. So what better explanation can be offered for how it happened? Unless we have missed something, there exists none. And if there exists none, we are invited to submit to the logic of what we now know: that this most celebrated and most scorned miracle of miracles actually happened—and, perhaps most miraculously of all, can even be understood to have happened."
–**Eric Metaxas**

"There was a time when only specialized Christian missionaries needed to be able to defend the gospel of Jesus Christ against the attacks of Islam. Today every Christian has an opportunity and obligation to present the gospel effectively and in Christian love to the Muslims who have permeated our Western society. When your neighbor, your mechanic, your favorite basketball player, your employer or employee, or even your children's friends could very well be Muslims, the need for proper understanding and an effective Christian witness is abundantly clear." –**Josh McDowell**

"If hell is your future, your best life is now. But if headed for heaven, your best life is still to come. If you're outside of Christ, in other words, this life is as good as it gets. But if you're in Christ, your pain in this world is the only pain you'll ever experience, and your struggles now are the only ones you'll ever endure." –**Colin Smith**

"The words "lifestyle evangelism" have come to mean to many that we merely live a Christian life, in the hope that some day sinners will be drawn to us. I believe more in "life-saving" evangelism. Who could stand passively on a river bank hoping a drowning person will be drawn to him so that he could then rescue him?" –**Ray Comfort**

"The Dead Sea Scrolls and thousands of other ancient copies of the Bible have allowed textual experts to recover the original text of the Bible. For critics to prove that our modern Bibles are no longer faithful to the original text, they would have to be able to point to ancient copies of the Bible and show us what they used to say, and then show that our modern Bibles say something different. Well, that's the very thing critics can't do. Because when you look at the ancient manuscript copies of the Bible, you find that our modern copies of the Bible say what the ancient manuscripts say." –**Charlie Campbell**

"You may be surprised to know that most critics are not prepared to defend their faith...Many people have never thought through their views and don't know why they hold them." –**Greg Koukl**

"If you believe what you like in the gospels, and reject what you don't like, it is not the gospel you believe, but yourself." –**Augustine**

"Apostasy can have far-reaching and disastrous effects on an entire congregation's spiritual health. When false teaching goes unchallenged, it breeds more confusion and draws still more shallow and insincere people into the fold. If not vigorously resisted, apostasy will spread like leaven through seminaries, denominations, missions agencies, and other Christian institutions. False teaching thus attacks the church like a parasite, affecting our corporate testimony, inoculating people against the real truth of the gospel, proliferating false and halfhearted "disciples," and filling the church with people who are actually unbelievers. By such means, entire churches and denominations have been taken over by apostasy...Whole denominations (even many where the gospel was once proclaimed clearly) have been left spiritually bankrupt because error and unbelief were tolerated rather than being opposed." –**John MacArthur**

"[Richard] Dawkins and his cohorts are always demanding evidence and asserting that there is no evidence for God. After all, we can't touch, see, hear, smell, or taste God, so why believe He exists? But then they ask us to believe in multiple universes that we can't touch, see, hear, smell, or taste either." –**Frank Turek**

"When Paul argued for the historicity of the physical resurrection, he said Jesus appeared to Peter and then the Twelve, and that "after that, he appeared to more than five hundred of the brothers at the same time, most of who are still living, though some have fallen asleep" (1 Corinthians 15:6). Paul tells his readers that the Resurrection could be verified by many eyewitnesses who were still living and encourages his reader to go and ask them about it!" –**Erwin Lutzer**

"Nothing, absolutely nothing, has a more direct bearing on the moral choices made by individuals or the purposes pursued by society than belief or disbelief in God." –**Ravi Zacharias**

"Most people who believe in the authority of the Bible did not come to this conviction through argument, but through encounter. For example, when soldiers were sent to arrest Jesus early in his ministry, they returned empty-handed. Why had they disobeyed orders? Because they had listened. "Never did a man speak the way this man speaks," they said (John 7:46). Jesus didn't start his discourse with reasons why people should believe his words. Instead, he simply spoke the truth, and it immediately resonated with many in the crowd." –**Greg Koukl**

"These are exciting times. When I finished the Epilogue to *Darwin on Trial* in 1993, I compared evolutionary naturalism to a great battleship afloat on the Ocean of Reality. The ship's sides are heavily armored with philosophical and legal barriers to criticism, and its decks are stacked with 16-inch rhetorical guns to intimidate would-be attackers. In appearance, it is as impregnable as the Soviet Union seemed a few years ago. But the ship has sprung a metaphysical leak, and that leak widens as more and more people understand it and draw attention to the conflict between empirical science and materialist philosophy. The more perceptive of the ship's officers know that the ship is doomed if the leak cannot be plugged. The struggle to save the ship will go on for a while, and meanwhile there will even be academic wine-and-cheese parties on the deck. In the end, the ship's great firepower and ponderous armor will only help drag it to the bottom. Reality will win." –**Phillip E. Johnson**

"Always remember that Jesus commanded His followers to go into the world and make disciples, not simply win arguments."
–**Andy Bannister**

"Scientists are slowly waking up to an inconvenient truth—the universe looks suspiciously like a fix. The issue concerns the very laws of nature themselves. For 40 years, physicists and cosmologists have been quietly collecting examples of all too convenient "coincidences" and special features in the underlying laws of the universe that seem to be necessary in order for life, and hence conscious beings, to exist. Change any one of them and the consequences would be lethal. Fred Hoyle, the distinguished cosmologist, once said it was as if 'a super-intellect has monkeyed with physics.'" –**Paul Davies**

"The cremated ashes of Siddhartha Guatama (now known as the Buddha) lay in a grave at the foot of the Himalayan Mountains. Muhammad, the founder of Islam, is buried in Medina, Saudi Arabia. Joseph Smith is buried in Nauvoo, Illinois. Charles Darwin is buried at Westminster Abbey in London. They are all dead and their graves are occupied. Only Jesus Christ proved that what He said was true by rising from the dead." –**Charlie Campbell**

"These days, though, tolerance means that you accept the other person's views as being true or legitimate. If you claim that someone is wrong, you can get accused of being intolerant—even though, ironically, the person making the charge of intolerance isn't being accepting of your beliefs." –**Paul Copan**

"Well, we are now about 120 years after Darwin and the knowledge of the fossil record has been greatly expanded. We now have a quarter of a million fossil species but the situation hasn't changed much. The record of evolution is still surprisingly jerky and, ironically, we have even fewer examples of evolutionary transitions than we had in Darwin's time. By this I mean that some of the classic cases of darwinian change in the fossil record, such as the evolution of the horse in North America, have had to be discarded or modified as a result of more detailed information—what appeared to be a nice simple progression when relatively few data were available now appear to be much more complex and much less gradualistic. So Darwin's problem has not been alleviated in the last 120 years and we still have a record which does show change but one that can hardly be looked upon as the most reasonable consequence of natural selection."
–**David Raup**

"Jesus is one of the very few persons in history who founded a great world religion or who, like Plato or Aristotle, has set the course of human thought and life for centuries. Jesus is in that tiny, select group. On the other hand, there have been a number of persons over the years who have implicitly or explicitly claimed to be divine beings from other worlds. Many of them were demagogues; many more were leaders of small, self-contained sects of true believers. What is unique about Jesus is that he is the only member of the first set of persons who is also a member of the second." –**Tim Keller**

"I often encounter devoted, committed Christians who are hesitant to embrace an evidential faith. In many Christian circles, faith that requires evidential support is seen as weak and inferior. For many, blind faith (a faith that simply trusts without question) is the truest, most sincere, and most valuable form of faith that we can offer God. Yet Jesus seemed to have a high regard for evidence. In John 14:11,

He told those watching Him to examine "the evidence of the miracles" if they did not believe what He said about His identity. Even after the resurrection, Jesus stayed with His disciples for an additional forty days and provided them with "many convincing proofs" that He was resurrected and was who He claimed to be (Acts 1:2–3). Jesus understood the role and value of evidence and the importance of developing an evidential faith." –**J. Warner Wallace**

"How is it that people instinctively know that something is either right or wrong? In order for humans to know the difference between right and wrong, there must be an objective standard beyond or independent of the human race. There cannot be a law without a lawgiver. Evidence suggests that there is a universal moral law; therefore, there must be a moral lawgiver, namely, God."
–**Norman Geisler** and **Ryan Snuffer**

"Someone once said that if you sat a million monkeys at a million typewriters for a million years, one of them would eventually type out all of Hamlet by chance. But when we find the text of Hamlet, we don't wonder whether it came from chance and monkeys. Why then does the atheist use that incredibly improbable explanation for the universe? Clearly, because it is his only chance of remaining an atheist. At this point we need a psychological explanation of the atheist rather than a logical explanation of the universe." –**Peter Kreeft**

"Truth that is not undergirded by love makes the truth obnoxious and the possessor of it repulsive." –**Ravi Zacharias**

"I have been used for many years to study the histories of other times and to examine and weigh the evidence of those who have written about them, and I know of no one fact in the history of mankind which is proved by better and fuller evidence of every sort, to the understanding of a fair inquirer, than the great sign which God hath given us that Christ died and rose again from the dead."
–**Thomas Arnold**

"I think that we're guided by the motto in "essentials unity, non-es-

sentials liberty and in all things charity." So if pastors compromise essential Christian doctrine, I think that there is a biblical warrant for naming them. Just as there [was] a practical warrant for calling out Tylenol [when] it was laced with cyanide. You had to name names. It was for the good of people and when there are ministers who are communicating or dispensing spiritual cyanide by the mega dose—I think that it's proper to warn people when they have clearly crossed the line between the Kingdom of Christ and the kingdom of the cults."
–**Hank Hanegraaff**

"I remember how frustrated I became when, as a young atheist, I examined specimens under the microscope. I would often walk away and try to convince myself that I was not seeing examples of extraordinary design, but merely the product of some random, unexplained mutations." –**Rick Oliver**

"The main reason Scripture does not directly address the issue of abortion is that abortion was so unimaginable to an Israelite woman it was not even necessary to mention it in the legal code. For one thing, children were considered a blessing from God (Ps. 127:3). Second, God is the sovereign ruler over conception in the womb (Gen. 29:33; 1 Sam. 1:19–20). And third, it was viewed as a curse to remain childless (Deut. 25:6). The Bible is silent about abortion because it was unthinkable in the Hebrew mind." –**Sean McDowell**

"Christianity is not based on feelings, or wishful thinking, but on real historical events reported by eyewitnesses" –**Andy Bannister**

"When it comes to the whole debate today over evolution versus creation, Jesus affirmed the early chapters of Genesis were accurate when He said, "Have you not read, that He who created them from the beginning made them male and female" (Matthew 19:4). Adam and Eve didn't come on the scene after billions of years of mutations and evolution. No. God created them all the way back in the beginning—just like Moses reported in the Book of Genesis."
–**Charlie Campbell**

"The pronouncement of the death penalty on Adam was both a curse and a blessing. A curse because death is horrible and continually reminds us of the ugliness of sin; a blessing because it meant the consequences of sin—separation from fellowship with God—need not be eternal. Death stopped Adam and his descendants from living in a state of sin, with all its consequences, forever." –**Ken Ham**

"It is fashionable in some academic circles to exercise scholarly criticism of the Bible. In so doing, scholars place themselves above the Bible and seek to correct it. If indeed the Bible is the Word of God, nothing could be more arrogant. It is God who corrects us; we don't correct Him. We do not stand over God but under Him."
–**R.C. Sproul**

"A good apologist is not just one who has all the right answers. He is also a person who communicates those answers in a God-honoring way." –**Ron Rhodes**

"Holy Scripture could never lie or err...its decrees are of absolute and inviolable truth." –**Galileo Galilei**

"We have got to start talking differently about "faith." Unfortunately, we have let the secular world and antagonists like Bill Maher define the term for us. What they mean by "faith" is blind leaping. That is what they think our commitment to Christ and the Christian view of the world is all about. They think we have simply disengaged our minds and leapt blindly into the religious abyss. The biblical view of saving Christian faith has never had anything to do with blind leaping. Jesus himself was fixed on the idea that we can know the truth—and not just in some spiritual or mystical way. Rather, he taught that we can know the truth about God, humans, and salvation objectively. That is, the very best forms of investigation, evidence, and careful reasoning will inevitably point to God and His great plans for us"
–**Craig Hazen**

"The Bible is God's declaratory revelation to man containing the great truths about God, about man, about history, about salvation, and about prophecy that God wanted us to know. The Bible could be trusted just as much as if God had taken the pen and written the words Himself." –**John Walvoord**

"Due to the enormous amounts of information and the machine-like complexity and interconnectedness of biological systems, atheists such as Francis Crick, Fred Hoyle, Stephen Hawking, and even Richard Dawkins have suggested that aliens could be responsible for seeding our planet with life. The theory is called panspermia, meaning seeds everywhere. Google it. Why are these men open to the designer being an alien but not God?" –**Frank Turek**

"Stephen Hawking said, 'religion is a fairy story for people afraid of the dark.' I said, 'atheism is a fairy story for people afraid of the light.'" –**John Lennox**

"The Bible is the Word of God, and God cannot err. So, to deny inerrancy, rightly understood, is to attack the very character of God. Those who deny inerrancy, soon enter the dangerous terrain of denying all Scriptural authority for both doctrine and practice."
–**Ravi Zacharias**

"There is a zero–tolerance policy for any tampering with the gospel. Contending for the purity of the gospel is a hill worth dying on."
–**Steven Lawson**

"The *Encyclopedia Britannica*, fifteenth edition, devotes 20,000 words to the person of Jesus Christ and never once hints that He didn't exist." –**John Ankerberg**

"I think that it is so important to know this. In a time like this of tolerance, listen, false teaching will always cry intolerance. It will always say you are being divisive, you are being unloving, you are being ungracious, because it can only survive when it doesn't get scrutinized. So it cries against any intolerance. It cries against any examination, any scrutiny—just let's embrace each other; let's love each other; let's put all that behind us. False doctrine cries the loudest about unity.

Listen carefully when you hear the cry for unity, because it may be the cover of false doctrine encroaching. If ever we should follow 1 Thessalonians 5, and examine everything carefully, it's when somebody is crying unity, love, and acceptance." –**John MacArthur**

"The greatest shame isn't disbelieving Hell exists, but in believing while making little effort to keep others from going there."
–**Randy Alcorn**

"Jesus said that one of the ways to find out whether He was speaking the truth was by first choosing to do God's will. He said, "If anyone is willing to do His will, he will know of the teaching, whether it is of God or whether I speak from Myself" (John 7:17). One of the reasons some people aren't sure about the truthfulness of Jesus's words is because they're not concerned with pleasing God. They are living for themselves. If they were to purpose in their hearts to live a life pleasing to God and then pick up the New Testament and read it, I'm convinced many of them would come to the realization that Jesus spoke the truth." –**Charlie Campbell**

"The main reason for insisting on the universal Flood as a fact of history and as the primary vehicle for geological interpretation is that God's Word plainly teaches it! No geologic difficulties, real or imagined, can be allowed to take precedence over the clear statements and necessary inferences of Scripture." –**Henry Morris**

"We have only to see a few letters of the alphabet spelling our name in the sand to recognize at once the work of an intelligent agent. How much more likely, then is the existence of an intelligent Creator behind human DNA, the colossal biological database that contains no fewer than 3.5 billion "letters"—the longest "word" yet discovered?"
–**John Lennox**

"In short, I didn't become a Christian because God promised I would have an even happier life than I had as an atheist. He never promised any such thing. Indeed, following him would inevitably bring divine demotions in the eyes of the world. Rather, I became a Christian because the evidence was so compelling that Jesus really is the one-and-only Son of God who proved his divinity by rising from the dead. That meant following him was the most rational and logical step I could possibly take." –**Lee Strobel**

Someone once asked Billy Graham, "If Christianity is valid, why is there so much evil in the world?" To this the famous preacher replied, "With so much soap, why are there so many dirty people in the world? Christianity, like soap, must be personally applied if it is to make a difference in our lives." –**Billy Graham**

"[Reason tells me of the] extreme difficulty or rather impossibility of conceiving this immense and wonderful universe, including man with his capability of looking far backwards and far into futurity, as the result of blind chance or necessity. When thus reflecting I feel compelled to look to a First Cause having an intelligent mind in some degree analogous to that of man; and I deserve to be called a Theist." –**Charles Darwin**

"Whatever has a beginning has a cause. Science shows us that the universe had a beginning. It therefore had a cause—one that's outside of itself and is therefore beyond time, space, matter, and physical energy. In other words, that cause has the characteristics of the God of the Bible." –**Mark Mittelberg**

"I claim to be an historian. My approach to Classics is historical. And I tell you that the evidence for the life, the death, and the resurrection of Christ is better authenticated than most of the facts of ancient history." –**E.M. Blaiklock**

"Unsophisticated religious pluralism responds to the religious diversity of mankind by saying, "Well, they are all true! All of the world's religions are basically saying the same thing." This view, which you very often find on the lips of college sophomores and laypeople, just evinces, frankly, tremendous ignorance of the teachings of the world's great religions. Anybody who has studied even a little bit of comparative religion knows that the worldviews that are propounded by these different religions are diametrically opposed to each other. Therefore, they cannot all be true." –**William Craig**

"A Chinese paleontologist lectures around the world saying that recent fossil finds in his country are inconsistent with the Darwinian theory of evolution. His reason: The major animal groups appear abruptly in the rocks over a relatively short time, rather than evolving gradually from a common ancestor as Darwin's theory predicts. When this conclusion upsets American scientists, he wryly comments: "In China we can criticize Darwin but not the government. In America you can criticize the government but not Darwin."
–**Phillip E. Johnson**

"God has provided enough evidence in this life to convince anyone willing to believe, yet he has also left some ambiguity so as not to compel the unwilling." –**Norman Geisler**

"If the solar system was brought about by an accidental collision, then the appearance of organic life on this planet was also an accident, and the whole evolution of Man was an accident too. If so, then all our thought processes are mere accidents—the accidental by-product of the movement of atoms. And this holds for the materialists' and astronomers' as well as for anyone else's. But if their thoughts—i.e., of Materialism and Astronomy—are merely accidental by-products, why should we believe them to be true? I see no reason for believing that one accident should be able to give a correct account of all the other accidents." –**C.S. Lewis**

"What did the Jewish New Testament writers have to gain by making up a new religion? By insisting the Resurrection occurred, they got excommunicated from the synagogue and then beaten, tortured, and killed. Last I checked that was not a list of perks." –**Frank Turek**

"When a denomination begins to consider doctrine divisive, theology troublesome, and convictions inconvenient, consider that denomination on its way to a well-deserved death." –**Albert Mohler**

"Even if the disciples had believed in the resurrection of Jesus, it is doubtful they would have generated any following. So long as the body was interred in the tomb, a Christian movement founded on belief in the resurrection of the dead man would have been an impossible folly." –**William Craig**

"Just who has imposed on the suffering human race poison gas, barbed wire, high explosives, experiments in eugenics, the formula for Zyklon B, heavy artillery, pseudo–scientific justifications for mass murder, cluster bombs, attack submarines, napalm, intercontinental ballistic missiles, military space platforms, and nuclear weapons? If memory serves, it was not the Vatican." –**David Berlinski**

"Born in the East and clothed in Oriental form and imagery, the Bible walks the ways of all the world with familiar feet and enters land after land to find its own everywhere. It has learned to speak in hundreds of languages to the heart of man. Children listen to its stories with wonder and delight, and wise men at its warnings, but to the wounded and penitent it has a mother's voice. It has woven itself into our dearest dreams; so that love, friendship, sympathy, devotion, memory, hope, put on the beautiful garments of its treasured speech. No man is poor or desolate who has this treasure for his own. When the landscape darkens, and the trembling pilgrim comes to the Valley of the Shadow, he is not afraid to enter; he takes the rod and staff of Scripture in his hand; he says to friend and comrade, 'Goodbye; we shall meet again'; and confronted by that support, he goes toward the lonely pass as one who walks through darkness into light." –**Henry Van Dyke**

"Some people say, 'There's no evidence God exists!' but when asked, 'What are some of the books you've read that lay out a case for God?'—Crickets! Most are not looking for God or considering the evidence. They are running from God. They're looking for God about as much as a criminal is looking for a police officer."
–**Charlie Campbell**

"If all the evidence is weighed carefully and fairly, it is indeed justifiable, according to the canons of historical research, to conclude that the sepulcher of Joseph of Arimathea, in which Jesus was buried, was actually empty on the morning of the first Easter. And no shred of evidence has yet been discovered in literary sources, epigraphy, or archaeology that would disprove this statement." –**Paul Maier**

"The charge that belief in God is irrational is common, but completely without basis. I'm not going to let anyone who makes this assertion off easily. I want to know, specifically, how theism is at odds with good thinking...Believing in leprechauns is irrational. Believing in God, by contrast, is like believing in atoms. The process is exactly the same. You follow the evidence of what you can see to conclude the existence of something you cannot see. The effect needs a cause adequate to explain it. There is nothing irrational or unreasonable about the idea of a personal God creating the material universe. A Big Bang needs a "big Banger," it seems to me. A complex set of instructions (as in DNA) needs an author. A blueprint requires an engineer. A moral law needs a moral lawgiver. This is not a leap; it is a step of intelligent reflection. Therefore, the question "Specifically, what is irrational about believing in God?" is completely in order."
–**Greg Koukl**

"They [the disciples] were testifying to the resurrection, a question of fact, not merely of faith. They were convinced of an event. And their willingness to die for attesting to that event is far more convincing than the willingness of others to die for a mere belief or because of loyalty to a religion or religious leader." –**Dave Hunt**

"What makes you so sure that God exists at all—especially when you can't see, hear, or touch him? We believe in many things that we don't see or directly experience with our senses—the virtue of love being a great example. Yet we see evidence of love through its effects. Similarly, we can't see God, but we can believe in him based on his work in us and in the universe around us." –**Mark Mittelberg**

"A single living cell is the most complex known machine in the universe, except, of course, for the life forms made up of numbers of cells." –**Jeffrey Russell**

"When I began speaking on college campuses in the 1960s there was a general commitment that truth could be found. But now people question the very existence and knowability of truth. There's also an assumption in the minds of many people that Christianity itself is bad and that Christians are bigots. Thus, before we can persuade people with the evidence that Jesus is the truth (John 14:6), we need to first address some of these misconceptions." –**Josh McDowell**

"Science rightfully enjoys great prestige in our society. But it's a mistake to believe that every question can be answered by that same kind of science. As mentioned earlier, knowing how nature operates is not the same as knowing how nature originated." –**Frank Turek**

"All laws legislate morality. The only question is whose morals will be legislated and which viewpoint will be advanced." –**Alan Shlemon**

"I saw a young sister, just before this service; and I said to her, "When did you find the Lord?" She replied, "It was when I was very ill." Yes, it is often so; God makes us ill in body that we may have time to think of Him, and turn to Him...What would become of some people if they were always in good health, or if they were always prospering? But tribulation is the black dog that goes after the stray sheep, and barks them back to the Good Shepherd. I thank God that there are such things as the visitations of correction and of holy discipline, to preserve our spirit, and bring us to Christ." –**Charles Spurgeon**

"When you analyze all of the most current affirmative evidence from cosmology, physics, astronomy, biology, and so forth...the positive case for an intelligent designer becomes absolutely compelling."
–**Jonathan Wells**

"Either God exists, or he does not...Let us weigh the gain and the loss in betting that God exists...If you win, you win everything; if you lose, you lose nothing. Do not hesitate then, to gamble on His existence." –**Blaise Pascal**

"When people begin religious movements, it's often not until many generations later that people record things about them, but the fact is that we have better historical documentation for Jesus than for the founder of any other ancient religion...[it's] quite impressive in terms of how much we can learn about him aside from the New Testament." –**Edwin Yamauchi**

"God speaks to man through the Scriptures, and He does not reveal normative truth except as it is already revealed in the Scriptures themselves. The test of truth must remain not what man experiences today but what the Scriptures have stated long ago." –**John Walvoord**

"It never ceases to amaze us that when we were in kindergarten they taught us that a frog turning into a prince was a nursery fairy tale, but when we got to college they told us that a frog turning into a prince was science." –**Ron Carlson** and **Ed Decker**

"A beast of a man killed 59 Americans [in Las Vegas in 2017] and wounded over 500 more. Now the fuss is all about gun control and the motive. The big picture that they never consider is that for over 50 years the kids in grade school to college have been taught that there is no great Creator God who is a God of justice and judgement. Life on earth came about by totally naturalistic means—evolution. Our ancestors are apes and reptiles. There is no absolute moral code. They are unwilling to consider that over time this can have a very bad effect on society. Consequently, the violence that we see now and that which is to come are going to become the inevitable norm."
–**Mace Baker**

"The fact that the first three Gospels were written prior to the fall of Jerusalem in A.D. 70 and the Gospel of John not long thereafter, makes impossible the attempt of liberal Bible critics and secularists to argue that they are the product of a developing oral tradition in which the early church modified Jesus' life and teachings."
–**John Warwick Montgomery**

"The most astounding thing God has ever done to show His existence to us is when He passed through the veil between heaven and earth and came to live among us as a man." –**Sue Bohlin**

"The reason some people reject Christianity is not due to their problems with one or two isolated Christian beliefs; their dissent results rather from the fact that their fundamentally anti-Christian worldview leads them to reject information and arguments that support the Christian worldview." –**Ronald Nash**

"There are those who teach that health and wealth are available from God virtually upon demand. If you are a Christian and you are suffering either physically or financially, the implication of this false doctrine is that you are in sin or you lack faith. Such religious condemnation toward man and attempted manipulation of God is contrary to God's word. Even the Apostle Paul had to endure a great physical affliction, "a thorn in the flesh." This mighty man of faith earnestly sought the Lord three times for relief. Paul had often witnessed God's healing grace. On this occasion, he was to learn of God's sustaining grace. "And He said to me, My grace is sufficient for you, for My strength is made perfect in weakness" (2 Corinthians 12:9). Many times the Lord works in and through our lives more powerfully in sustaining us through difficulties than He does by removing them. The financial promises of the 'Health and Wealth Gospel' represent a further perversion of the Scriptures. If we heeded the warnings of 1 Timothy 6:6–10, these enticing and seductive deceptions regarding wealth would lose their appeal. "Now godliness with contentment is great gain...And having food and clothing, with these we shall be content...but those who desire to be rich fall into temptation and a snare...for the love of money is a root of all kinds of evil, for which some have strayed from the faith in their greediness."
–**Bob Hoekstra**

"Atheist: If you were born in Iraq, you wouldn't be a Christian. Christian: If you were born in Iraq, you wouldn't be an atheist. Now what?" –**Greg Koukl**

"Many years later, however, I read the New Testament for myself. The

Jesus I encountered was far different from the deluded radical, even mythical character described to me. This Jesus—the Jesus of history—was real. He touched upon things that cut close to my heart, especially as I pondered the meaning of human existence. I was struck by the early church's testimony to Jesus: In Christ's death God has vanquished evil, and by his resurrection he has brought life and hope to all." –**Michael Bird**

"God whispers to us in our pleasures, speaks in our conscience, but shouts in our pains. It is his megaphone to rouse a deaf world."
–**C.S. Lewis**

"The virgin birth of the Messiah was not plagiarized from some other religion, as some critics contend. It was the fulfillment of a prophecy given in the Old Testament book of Isaiah six or seven hundred years before Jesus's birth. And many Bible commentators believe the virgin birth of the Messiah was prophesied as far back as Genesis 3 where God seems to indicate that the coming Messiah would be born solely of the woman's seed." –**Charlie Campbell**

"It now seems to me that the findings of more than fifty years of DNA research have provided materials for a new and enormously powerful argument to design." –**Antony Flew**

"The tooth of time gnaws all books but the Bible...Nineteen centuries of experience have tested it. It has passed through critical fires no other volume has suffered, and its spiritual truths have endured the flames and come out without so much as the smell of burning."
–**W.E. Sangster**

"One of the most modern pretenders to inspiration is the Book of Mormon. I could not blame you should you laugh outright while I read aloud a page from that farrago." –**Charles Spurgeon**

"The Bible encourages people to put their faith in God. Unfortunately, many people equate faith with a blind leap in the dark or wishful thinking. But the faith that the Bible requires is intelligent faith. It

is neither blind nor irrational. Biblical faith is a committing trust with an object (God) who is worthy of our faith. No one is asked to sacrifice his intellect when he puts his faith in the God of the Bible."
–Don Stewart

"A common sense interpretation of the facts suggests that a super-intellect has monkeyed with physics, as well as with chemistry and biology, and that there are no blind forces worth speaking about in nature. The numbers one calculates from the facts seem to me so overwhelming as to put this conclusion almost beyond question."
–Fred Hoyle

"Just because something is unseen doesn't mean it's not real. There are many unseen realities that scientists use every day, such as the laws of logic, the laws of mathematics, the laws of nature, their minds, and so forth. And scientists infer from the effects they do see to causes they don't see. John Lennox observes, "Postulating an unobserved Designer is no more unscientific than postulating unobserved macroevolutionary steps." **–Frank Turek**

"Truth is never determined by looking at God's Word and asking, "What does this mean to me?" Whenever I hear someone talk like that, I'm inclined to ask, "What did the Bible mean before you existed? What does God mean by what He says?" Those are the proper questions to be asking. Truth and meaning are not determined by our intuition, experience, or desire. The true meaning of Scripture—or anything else, for that matter—has already been determined and fixed by the mind of God. The task of the interpreter is to discern that meaning. And proper interpretation must precede application."
–John MacArthur

"What is often not appreciated by unbelievers is the fact that the felt need for God is not limited to unthinking and uncritical religious people. Some of the greatest minds, including the founders of most areas of modern science, confessed their need. Not surprisingly this list includes theologians Augustine, Anselm, and Thomas Aquinas. But it also includes Galileo Galilei, Nicolaus Copernicus, William

Kelvin, Isaac Newton, Francis Bacon, Blaise Pascal, Rene Descartes, Gottfried Leibniz, John Locke, and Soren Kierkegaard. One can hardly claim that intellectual deficiency led to their perceived need for God." –**Norman Geisler**

"But what if Jesus had never been born? What difference would it have made if a Bethlehem stable had never served as a makeshift delivery room? A great deal. Jesus, the greatest man who ever lived, has changed virtually every aspect of human life. Much of what we take for granted—our high regard for human life, the elevation of women, education, science, charity, hospitals, capitalism, the abolition of slavery, representative government, literacy, and the development of art and music—all find their roots in Christ and His teachings."
–**D. James Kennedy**

"The temptation to believe that the universe is the product of some sort of design, a manifestation of subtle aesthetic and mathematical judgment, is overwhelming. The belief that there is "something behind it all" is one that I personally share with, I suspect, a majority of physicists." –**Paul Davies**

"I am an historian, I am not a believer, but I must confess as a historian that this penniless preacher from Nazareth is irrevocably the very center of history. Jesus Christ is easily the most dominant figure in all history." –**H.G. Wells**

"Atheism is a crutch for those who cannot bear the reality of God."
–**Tom Stoppard**

"Fundamentally, our Lord's message was Himself. He did not come merely to preach a Gospel; He himself is that Gospel. He did not come merely to give bread; He said, "I am the bread." He did not come merely to shed light; He said, "I am the light." He did not come merely to show the door; He said, "I am the door." He did not come merely to name a shepherd; He said, "I am the shepherd." He did not come merely to point the way; He said, "I am the way, the truth, and the life." –**J. Sidlow Baxter**

"Raking all the evidence together, it is not too much to say that there is no historic incident better or more variously supported than the resurrection of Christ. Nothing but the antecedent assumption that it must be false could have suggested the idea of deficiency in the proof of it." –**Brooke Westcott**

"Evolution is unobservable. It's based on blind faith in a few dry bones and on unreliable dating systems in which the gullible trust. Kids should be allowed to make up their own minds about this issue, and not be censored to 'one side is all we will let you hear.'"
–**Ray Comfort**

"If God became incarnate, what kind of man would He be?...We would expect Him to be sinless; we would expect him to be holy; we would expect His words to be the greatest words ever spoken; we would expect Him to exert a profound power over human personality; we would expect Him to perform supernatural doings; and we would expect Him to manifest the love of God. Of all human beings who have ever lived, Jesus Christ alone met all of those criteria."
–**John MacArthur** and **Bernard Ramm**

"Another point important to recognize is that the creation was 'mature' from its birth. It did not have to grow or develop from simple beginnings. God formed it full–grown in every respect, including even Adam and Eve as mature individuals when they were first formed. The whole universe had an 'appearance of age' right from the start. It could not have been otherwise for true creation to have taken place. 'Thus the heavens and the earth were finished, and all the host of them' (Genesis 2:1)." –**Henry Morris**

"Many of the challenging objections to the faith can be answered in under a minute or two. Don't think you need to have a Ph.D. to "contend for the faith" (Jude 1:3)." –**Charlie Campbell**

"Jesus of Nazareth, without money and arms, conquered more millions than Alexander, Caesar, Mohammed, and Napoleon; without science and learning, He shed more light on things human and di-

vine than all philosophers and schools combined; without the eloquence of schools, He spoke words of life such as never were spoken before or since, and produced effects which lie beyond the reach of any orator or poet; without writing a single line, He has set more pens in motion, and furnished themes for more sermons, orations, discussions, learned volumes, works of art and sweet songs of praise, than the whole army of great men of ancient and modern times."
–Philip Schaff

"The most beautiful system of the sun, planets and comets could only proceed from the counsel and dominion of an intelligent and powerful being." **–Isaac Newton**

"The world is witnessing a huge explosion of religious conversion and growth, and Christianity is growing faster than any other religion. Nietzsche's proclamation "God is dead" is now proven false. Nietzsche is dead. The ranks of the unbelievers are shrinking as a proportion of the world's population. Secularism has lost its identification with progress and modernity, and consequently it has lost the main source of its appeal. God is very much alive, and His future prospects look to be excellent. This is the biggest comeback story of the twenty-first century. If God is back, why don't we see it? The reason is that many of us live in the wrong neighborhood."
–Dinesh D'Souza

"The Gnostic Gospels are 2nd century (and later) gnostic texts that claim to be written by close followers of Jesus such as Mary, Peter, Thomas, and Judas. Although they're called "Gospels," they're actually quite dissimilar than Matthew, Mark, Luke, and John in both style and content. The Gospel of Thomas, for instance, is not a narrative, but 114 sayings attributed to Jesus. The reason these so-called "Gospels" are not in the Bible is because they're dated much later than the canonical Gospels, and they also contain teachings that fail to match up with what we know about the historical Jesus from the earliest sources (see Luke 1:1–4)." **–Sean McDowell**

"DNA is like a computer program, but far, far more advanced that any software we've ever created." –**Bill Gates**

"I must say, that having for many years made the evidences of Christianity the subject of close study, the result has been a firm and increasing conviction of the authenticity and plenary inspiration of the Bible. It is indeed the Word of God." –**Simon Greenleaf**

"If Darwinism is true, then there is no purpose or meaning to life, there is no morality, there's no qualitative difference between humans and animals, there's no life after death, and there's no purpose to human history. Now, are you trying to tell me that it doesn't really matter if people believe we evolved or not?" –**Greg Koukl**

"Here is a man [Jesus] who was born in an obscure village, the child of a peasant woman. He grew up in another village. He worked in a carpenter shop until He was thirty. Then for three years He was an itinerant preacher. He never owned a home. He never wrote a book. He never held an office. He never had a family. He never went to college. He never put His foot inside a big city. He never traveled two hundred miles from the place He was born. He never did one of the things that usually accompany greatness. He had no credentials but Himself...While still a young man, the tide of popular opinion turned against him. His friends ran away. One of them denied Him. He was turned over to His enemies. He went through the mockery of a trial. He was nailed upon a cross between two thieves. While He was dying, His executioners gambled for the only piece of property He had on earth—His coat. When He was dead, He was laid in a borrowed grave through the pity of a friend. Nineteen long centuries have come and gone, and today He is a centerpiece of the human race and leader of the column of progress. I am far within the mark when I say that all the armies that ever marched, all the navies that were ever built; all the parliaments that ever sat and all the kings that ever reigned, put together, have not affected the life of man upon this earth as powerfully as has that one solitary life." –**Author Unknown**

"Scientists who utterly reject evolution may be one of our fastest-growing controversial minorities...Many of the scientists supporting this position hold impressive credentials in science." –**Larry Hatfield**

"If there is a root of evil that became a terrifying force that almost brought the world to destruction in the first half of the twentieth century, it is the anti-religious ideologies of Germany and Russia, North Vietnam, and North Korea. It takes almost willful blindness to invert this historical fact, and to suppose that the religions that were persecuted and crushed by these brutal forces are the real sources of evil in the world...So the value judgment put forth by atheists that "atheism is good and Christianity is evil" is not only logically faulty because good and evil don't exist in an atheistic world—it's also empirically false!" –**Keith Ward** and **Frank Turek**

"A good apologist is a loving apologist (see 1 Corinthians 13:1). Love helps to bring down barriers to communication, whereas in-your-face apologetics erects those barriers. By using love in our apologetics, we are reflecting God's own character. Jesus Himself was love incarnate. We are ambassadors for Christ (2 Corinthians 5:20), so we ought to represent His love to others." –**Ron Rhodes**

"This belief that the universe created itself is fraught with problems. The idea that anything could create itself is absurd. For it would have to exist and not exist at the same time. Friends, that's irrational. For something to create itself, it would have to be before it was. Well, this violates an ironclad law of knowledge: the law of non-contradiction that states: A cannot be both A and non-A at the same time and in the same relationship. For example, you can't be at church right now and not at church right now. You are either here or not here. So then, it's absurd to suggest that the universe existed (A) and didn't exist (non-A) at the same time. But that is precisely what would be required for the universe to have created itself. So surely, the universe did not create itself." –**Charlie Campbell**

"In one sense, God doesn't send anyone to hell; we send ourselves. Hell is the culmination of telling God to "get out." You keep telling God to leave you alone, and finally God says, "Okay." That's why the Bible describes it as darkness: God is light; his absence is darkness.

On earth we experience light and things like love, friendship, and the beauty of creation. These are all remnants of the light of God's presence. But when you tell God you don't want him as the Lord and center of your life, eventually you get your wish, and with God go all of his gifts. We have two options: live with God, or live without God. If you say, "I don't want God's authority. I would rather live for myself," that's hell." –**J.D. Greaar**

"Please don't tell me Hitler was a Christian...it's completely contrary to the facts. Hitler may have used religious language for political gain. But does anyone really think that Hitler was sincerely and consistently worshipping a Jew whose guiding principle was to love God and your neighbor as yourself? Whatever Hitler believed, it wasn't orthodox Christianity." –**Frank Turek**

The skeptic asks, "Why posit an intelligent cause (designer) of the world when chance can explain the apparent design? Given enough time, any "lucky" combination will result. The universe may be a 'happy accident.'" For one thing, there has not been enough time for chance to work. One former atheist, Fred Hoyle, calculated that, given the geological time span of billions of years, the chances are still only one to $10^{30,000}$ that so complex a form as even a one-celled animal would emerge by purely natural forces (Hoyle). The chances are virtually zero that chance was responsible. Second, chance does not "cause" anything; only forces do. And it is known that natural forces do not produce specified complexity, such as that found in living things. Chance is only an abstraction that describes the intersection of two or more lines of causes. Finally, it is unscientific and irrational to appeal to chance. As even the skeptic David Hume noted, science is based on observation about regularly recurring events. And the only kind of cause known to rational beings that can cause the specified complexity found in living things is an intelligent cause."
–**Norman Geisler**

"In the whole history of the world, there is only one person who not only claimed to be God himself but also got enormous numbers of people to believe it. Only Jesus combines claims of divinity with the most beautiful life of humanity." –**Tim Keller**

"I remember Christian teachers telling me long ago that I must hate a bad man's actions but not hate the bad man: or, as they would say, hate the sin but not the sinner...I used to think this a silly, straw-splitting distinction: how could you hate what a man did and not hate the man? But years later it occurred to me that there was one man to whom I had been doing this all my life—namely myself. However much I might dislike my own cowardice or conceit or greed, I went on loving myself. There had never been the slightest difficulty about it. In fact the very reason why I hated the things was that I loved the man. Just because I loved myself, I was sorry to find that I was the sort of man who did those things." –**C.S. Lewis**

"That a few simple men should in one generation have invented so powerful and appealing a personality, so lofty an ethic, and so inspiring a vision of human brotherhood, would be a miracle far more incredible than any recorded in the Gospels. After two centuries of Higher Criticism the outlines of life, character, and teaching of Christ remain reasonably clear, and constitute the most fascinating feature in the history of Western man." –**Will Durant**

"Despite Hell's unpopularity these days, there are numerous references in the New Testament that warn of Hell and the judgment that awaits the unrighteous. The Bible describes "Hell" as a place of outer darkness (Mtt. 25:30), weeping (Mtt. 8:12), wailing (Mtt. 13:42), gnashing of teeth (Mtt. 13:50), flames (Lk. 16:24), everlasting fire (Mtt. 25:46), a furnace of fire (Mtt. 13:42), separation from the righteous (Mtt. 25:46), eternal destruction, away from the presence of the Lord (2 Thess. 1:9), torment (Lk. 16:23), everlasting punishment (Mtt. 25:46), and the lake of fire burning with brimstone (Rev. 19:20). The Bible seems to exhaust the human language describing just how awful of a place Hell will be. Who said these things about Hell? Peter? No. Luke? No. All but two of these descriptions were uttered by Jesus Himself." –**Charlie Campbell**

"Instinctively we do not class Him with others. When one reads His name in a list beginning with Confucius and ending with Goethe we feel it is an offense less against orthodoxy than against decency. Jesus is not one of the group of the world's great. Talk about Alexander the Great and Charles the Great and Napoleon the Great if you will…Jesus is apart. He is not the Great; He is the Only. He is simply Jesus…. He confounds our canons of human nature." –**Carnegie Simpson**

"The evidence for the truthfulness and historicity of the Bible continues to mount up as never before. Just when skepticism seems to be making the most noise, we are being flooded with an overwhelming amount of real, hard evidences that demand a verdict opposite to what skeptics…are clamoring for in their current worldviews and life views." –**Walter Kaiser**

"So I cast my lot with Him—not the one who claimed wisdom, Confucius; or the one who claimed enlightenment, Buddha; or the one who claimed to be a prophet, Muhammad, but with the one who claimed to be God in human flesh. The one who declared, 'Before Abraham was born, I am'—and proved it." –**Norman Geisler**

"Our Lord [Jesus] used historical incidents in the Old Testament in a manner that showed His total confidence in their factual historicity. He acknowledged that Adam and Eve were created by God, that they were two living human beings, not merely symbols of man and woman (Matt. 19:3–5; Mark 10:6–8)…He verified events connected with the flood of Noah's day (Matt. 24:38–39, Luke 17:26–27)…He authenticated God's destruction of Sodom and the historicity of Lot and his wife (Matt. 10:15; Luke 17:28–29). He accepted as true the story of Jonah and the great fish (Matt. 12:40)…Christ did not merely allude to these stories, but authenticated the events in them as factual history to be completely trusted. These events include many of the controversial passages of the Old Testament, such as Creation, the Flood, and major miracles including Jonah and the fish. Obviously, our Lord felt He had a reliable Bible, historically true, with every word trustworthy." –**Charles Ryrie**

"No evidence for God? Really? There's a difference between saying there's no evidence and saying the evidence offered isn't adequate or conclusive. If inadequate, to be fair you have to show why the evidence given isn't good and how your alternative explains the facts better." –**Greg Koukl**

"The Bible does acknowledge the reality of slavery in those times. A person could be taken as a slave if he was a prisoner of war, if he couldn't pay a debt, if he stole something that he couldn't repay, etc. However, there were laws governing how slaves could be treated and also ways they could gain their freedom. It's important to realize that we view the subject through the lens of American slavery, with its incredible cruelty. To be a slave in Bible times was more like being a modern–day servant. In fact, the Bible uses the word "bondservant" when referring to slaves, and instructs masters to treat them kindly (Eph. 6:5–9)." –**Ray Comfort**

"Scientific evidence has shown that "built into the natural development of children's minds [is] a predisposition to see the natural world as designed and purposeful and that some kind of intelligent being is behind that purpose." Even if a group of children were put "on an island and they raised themselves," Barrett adds, "I think they would believe in God." It appears that we have to be educated out of the knowledge of God by secular schools and media." –**Nancy Pearcey**

"Good defenders of the faith are good listeners. Good listeners shape their comments to fit the exact comments of the people with whom they are speaking. If we do not listen well, our follow–up questions will be off base and irrelevant." –**Ron Rhodes**

"Jehovah's Witnesses insist that the deity of Christ was a late invention by false teachers in the fourth century at the Council of Nicaea. Nothing could be further from the truth. In addition to the testimony of the Old Testament prophets (e.g., Isaiah 9:6), the disciples (e.g., John 20:28), and Christ Himself (John 8:58)—all who affirmed the deity of the Messiah—there is also the testimony of the church fathers in the second century, long before the Council of Nicaea. Men like Ignatius (A.D. 30 – 98 or 117), Justin Martyr (A.D. 100 – 165),

Irenaeus (A.D. 120–202), and Clement of Alexandria (A.D. 150 – 215) affirm over and over in their writings that Jesus was God incarnate." –**Charlie Campbell**

"Scientists have spent at least a century trying to create biological life from chemicals, yet they haven't made even one DNA molecule. Since a cell's energy, information storage, and metabolic machinery all depend on one another, the first cell could not have arisen through natural processes unless all three intricate systems sprang up at once. And besides that, body cells break down when they're not part of a living being. The universal failure of people to make life highlights God as the source of all life (Psalm 36:9)." –**Brian Thomas**

"I myself am convinced that the theory of evolution, especially the extent to which it's been applied, will be one of the great jokes in the history books in the future. Posterity will marvel that so very flimsy and dubious an hypothesis could be accepted with the incredible credulity that it has." –**Malcolm Muggeridge**

"Religion used to be the opium of the people. To those suffering humiliation, pain, illness, and serfdom, religion promised the reward of an after life. But now, we are witnessing a transformation, a true opium of the people is the belief in nothingness after death, the huge solace, the huge comfort of thinking that for our betrayals, our greed, our cowardice, our murders, we are not going to be judged."
–**Czeslaw Milosz**

"Many roads lead to Hell, but none that lead out. There is only one road that leads to Heaven, Jesus Christ." –**Steven Lawson**

[Why doesn't God just do something miraculous to prove He exists?] "God did bring down fire from Heaven on occasions (see Numbers 16:35; 1 Kings 18:38). He even opened the earth to swallow up his enemies (see Numbers 16:31–33). Did this result in people turning to him for the long run? No. Jesus fed the multitudes and many followed for a while, but they turned away recoiling from his demanding words (see John 6:1–66). Abraham told the rich man that his brothers "will not be convinced even if someone rises from the dead" (see Luke 16:27-31). We say, "Show me a miracle and I'll believe," yet countless people who have seen miracles continue to disbelieve. In our eagerness to see greater miracles, we regard "natural processes" as minor and secondary, missing God's marvelous daily interventions on our behalf. Focusing on God's "big miracles"—like curing cancer and making brain tumors disappear—causes us to overlook his small, daily miracles of providence in which he holds the universe together, provides us with air to breathe and lungs to breathe it, and food to eat and stomachs to digest it. Years ago when I became an insulin-dependent diabetic, it dawned on me that I had never once, in the fifteen years I'd known him, thanked God for a pancreas that had worked perfectly until then." –**Randy Alcorn**

"Postmodernism is a form of intellectual pacifism that, at the end of the day, recommends backgammon while the barbarians are at the gate. It is the easy, cowardly way out that removes the pressure to... be different, to risk ridicule, to take a stand outside the gate. But it is precisely as disciples of Christ, even more, as officers in His army, that the pacifist way out is simply not an option. However comforting it may be, postmodernism is the cure that kills the patient, the military strategy that concedes defeat before the first shot is fired, the ideology that undermines its own claims to allegiance. And it is an immoral, coward's way out that is not worthy of a movement born out of the martyrs' blood." –**J.P. Moreland**

"Even were the Qur'an a perfect word-for-word copy of the original as given by Muhammad, it would not prove the original was inspired of God. All it would demonstrate is that today's Qur'an is a carbon copy of whatever Muhammad said. It would say or prove nothing about the truth of what he said. The Muslim claim that they have the true religion, because they have the only perfectly copied holy book, is as logically fallacious as someone preferring a perfectly printed counterfeit $1000 bill over a slightly imperfect genuine one. The crucial question, which Muslim apologists beg by this argument, is whether the original is God's Word, not whether they possess a perfect copy of it." –**Norman Geisler**

"If you had gone to Buddha and asked him: 'Are you the son of Brahma?' he would have said, 'My son, you are still in the vale [valley] of illusion.' If you had gone to Socrates and asked, 'Are you Zeus?' he would have laughed at you. If you had gone to Mohammed and asked, 'Are you Allah?' he would first have rent his clothes and then cut your head off. If you had asked Confucius, 'Are you Heaven?' I think he would have probably replied, 'Remarks which are not in accordance with nature are in bad taste.' The idea of a great moral teacher saying what Christ said is out of the question. In my opinion, the only person who can say that sort of thing is either God or a complete lunatic..." –**C.S. Lewis**

"I came to Him because I did not know which way to turn. I remained with Him because there is no other way I wish to turn. I came to Him longing for something I did not have. I remain with Him because I have something I will not trade. I came to Him as a stranger. I remain with Him in the most intimate of friendships. I came to Him unsure about the future. I remain with Him certain about my destiny. I came amid the thunderous cries of a culture that has 330 million deities. I remain with Him knowing that truth cannot be all-inclusive." –**Ravi Zacharias**

"Hell's punishment [separation from God] fits sin's crime [i.e., it's not over-punishment] because sin is divorce from God. The punishment fits the crime because the punishment is the crime. Saying no to God means no God." –**Peter Kreeft**

"The puzzling question is not, "Why would God send good people to Hell?", but rather "Why would a just God allow bad people into Heaven?" –**Alan Sheldon**

"Why do people suppress the evidence for God? The God described in the Bible goes against the grain of today's popular notions of spirituality. Many people may be receptive to the idea of a non-personal spiritual force that they can tap into. They might be willing to consider a great pantheistic pool of spirituality of which they are a part. But they are far less comfortable with the concept of a living, active,

personal God who knows them, wants to interact with them, and has His own views about what they are doing with their lives."
–Nancy Pearcey

"Unless I am convinced by Scripture and plain reason—I do not accept the authority of the popes and councils, for they have contradicted each other—my conscience is captive to the Word of God. I cannot and I will not recant anything for to go against conscience is neither right nor safe. Here I stand. I can do no other. God help me. Amen." **–Martin Luther**

"I am often asked, 'Why do people continue to reject God, even after hearing of all this compelling evidence He exists?' Jesus explained one of the reasons when He said, "Men loved the darkness rather than the light, for their deeds were evil" (John 3:19). That's what's really going on in a lot of cases. It's rarely just an intellectual hang-up that keeps a person from believing in God." **–Charlie Campbell**

"The interesting thing about those who espouse various kinds of relativism: they all seem to end up by saying, essentially, that truth, perception, etc. are relative, except of course the truth they are passionately trying to get us to perceive. That is, they fail to apply their own relativism to themselves." **–John Lennox**

"Young Christians are getting barraged with tough questions about the faith at earlier rates than previous generations. As a result, many either compartmentalize their faith or abandon it entirely. If we want young people to hold firm to their faith in our increasingly secular culture, they need solid reasons." **–Josh McDowell**

"Atheism is not an absence of belief. It is a worldview with the positive beliefs that man is nothing but molecules and morality is subjective." **–Frank Turek**

"[Richard]Dawkins…appears to have placed himself in a difficult situation. He posits an amoral universe—one without intrinsic good and evil—precisely because no God exists. But if Dawkins wants to condemn Christians for immorality—*really* wants to condemn them—then it would seem that he must accept a moral universe, which would in turn demand a deity (since the lack of a deity is what characterizes it as amoral)." –**Scott Hahn** and **Benjamin Wiker**

"Many people are being persuaded that they cannot be considered intelligent or well educated if they insist on the doctrine of the verbal inspiration of the Book. Let me say to you that truth has always lived with the minority; what the majority says at a given moment is usually wrong. The crowd one day cried, "Crucify him," and the whole world united to murder the Son of God, because in their ignorance they knew Him not." –**Alan Redpath**

"Our Messiah sees himself as an expositor of Scripture, but never a corrector of Scripture. He fulfills it, but never falsifies it. He turns away wrong interpretations of Scripture, but insists there is nothing wrong with Scripture, down to the crossing of t's and dotting of i's."
–**Kevin DeYoung**

"According to Darwinists, there is such overwhelming evidence for their view that it should be considered a fact. Yet to the Darwinists' dismay, at least three-quarters of the American people—citizens of the most scientifically advanced country in history—reject it...The truth is Darwinism is not a scientific theory, but a materialistic creation myth masquerading as science. It is first and foremost a weapon against religion—especially traditional Christianity. Evidence is brought in afterwards, as window dressing. This is becoming increasingly obvious to the American people, who are not the ignorant backwoods religious dogmatists that Darwinists make them out to be. Darwinists insult the intelligence of American taxpayers and at the same time depend on them for support. This is an inherently unstable situation, and it cannot last." –**Jonathan Wells**

"There are those who hate Christianity and call their hatred an all-embracing love for all religions." –**G.K. Chesterton**

"As Paul stood on trial for preaching the resurrection of Jesus Christ, he asked those present a pointed question: "Why should any of you consider it incredible that God raises the dead (Acts 26:8)?" Many unbelievers find it too difficult, too incredible, that God would or could raise a dead man (Jesus) back to life. And yet, many of these same people have no problem believing that God exists and that He created the heavens and the earth. This is astonishing to me! Think this through with me. If God can create the universe with all its billions of galaxies, and millions of kinds of living creatures from nothing, it certainly seems within the bounds of reason to believe that He could raise Jesus's body back to life. As it has often been said, if you can believe Genesis 1:1, you should have no problem believing Matthew 28:6: 'He has risen, just as he said.'" –**Charlie Campbell**

"For me, apologetics proved to be the turning point of my life and eternity. I'm thankful for the scholars who so passionately and effectively defend the truth of Christianity—and today my life's goal is to do my part in helping others get answers to the questions that are blocking them in their spiritual journey toward Christ."
–**Lee Strobel**

"If the Resurrection had not occurred, why would the apostle Paul give such a list of supposed eyewitnesses? He would immediately lose all credibility with his Corinthian readers by lying so blatantly."
–**Norman Geisler** and **Frank Turek**

"The more examples of moral evil an atheist presents in support of his argument, the more evidence he's given that human beings are extremely sinful. And it makes little sense to say, 'Human beings are incredibly sinful and are at war with God, but God should give us a world of total pleasure and should rush to our aid whenever something goes wrong.'" –**David Wood**

"Archaeologists and other scholars have long probed the hemisphere's past, and the Society does not know of anything found so far that has substantiated the Book of Mormon."
–**The National Geographic Society**

"People may die for a lie they think is true, but they won't die for a lie they know to be false." –**Josh McDowell**

"There is an important difference between the apostle martyrs and those who die for their beliefs today. Modern martyrs act solely out of their trust in beliefs that others have taught them. The apostles died for holding to their own testimony that they had personally seen the risen Jesus. Contemporary martyrs die for what they believe to be true. The disciples of Jesus died for what they knew to be either true or false." –**Gary Habermas**

"The resurrection of Jesus Christ is the single greatest event in the history of the world. It is so foundational to Christianity that no one who denies it can be a true Christian. Without resurrection, there is no Christian faith, no salvation, and no hope. "If there is no resurrection of the dead," Paul explains, "not even Christ has been raised; and if Christ has not been raised, then our preaching is vain, your faith also is vain" (1 Cor. 15:13–14). A person who believes in a Christ who was not raised believes in a powerless Christ, a dead Christ. If Christ did not rise from the dead, then no redemption was accomplished at the cross and "your faith is worthless," Paul goes on to say; "you are still in your sins" (v. 17)." –**John MacArthur**

"Far from belief in God hindering science, it was the motor that drove it. Isaac Newton, when he discovered the law of gravitation, did not make the common mistake of saying: 'now I have a law of gravity, I don't need God'. Instead, he wrote *Principia Mathematica*, the most famous book in the history of science, expressing the hope that it would persuade the thinking man to believe in a Creator."
–**John Lennox**

"According to the laws of legal evidence used in courts of law, there is more evidence for the historical fact of the resurrection of Jesus Christ than for just about any other event in history."
–**Simon Greenleaf**

"Think of the Earth's incredible water cycle. Heat from the sun warms up salty, undrinkable ocean water. As the water evaporates, it leaves the salt behind and is transported into the atmosphere where it forms clouds. Then the winds blow the clouds over the continents. The water droplets then condense and fall to the earth and provide hydration to billions of humans and animals. Other droplets fall to the ground and awaken dormant seeds that produce an amazing variety of fruits and vegetables. And then the water begins its journey all over again. And it's been doing this over and over. Could this marvelous system have come about accidentally? No. The water cycle, the seeds, the fruit and vegetables point to a benevolent creator who loves us (see Acts 14:16–17.)" –**Charlie Campbell**

"The prochoice position always overlooks the victim's right to choose. Blacks didn't choose slavery. Jews didn't choose the ovens. Women don't choose rape. And babies don't choose abortion."
–**Randy Alcorn**

"I had to admit that the science I loved so much was powerless to answer questions such as "What is the meaning of life?" "Why am I here?" "Why does mathematics work, anyway?" "If the universe had a beginning, who created it?" "Why are the physical constants in the universe so finely tuned to allow the possibility of complex life forms?" "Why do humans have a moral sense?" "What happens after we die?"" –**Francis Collins**

"Jesus has in His bloodline two prostitutes (Tamar and Rahab), an adulterer (Bathsheba), and a King (David) who lies, cheats, and murders to cover up his sins. Who would have invented this? Do you think Matthew and Luke felt it was necessary to "spice up" the Messiah's bloodline with prostitutes, adulterers, and murderers?"
–**Frank Turek**

"Relativism poses as freedom but it is just another form of tyranny: You must believe that all religions are equal because we say they are. You must agree with us that everything is relative, or we will punish you." –**Jeffrey Russell**

"We [like-minded atheists] take the side of science in spite of the patent absurdity of some of its constructs, in spite of its failure to fulfill many of its extravagant promises of health and life, in spite of the tolerance of the scientific community for unsubstantiated just-so stories, because we have a prior commitment, a commitment to materialism. It is not that the methods and institutions of science somehow compel us to accept a material explanation of the phenomenal world, but, on the contrary, that we are forced by our a priori adherence to material causes to create an apparatus of investigation and a set of concepts that produce material explanations, no matter how counter-intuitive, no matter how mystifying to the uninitiated. Moreover, that materialism is absolute, for we cannot allow a Divine Foot in the door."
–**Richard Lewontin**

"The Bible says that God desires all men to be saved and to come to the knowledge of the truth (1 Tim. 2:4; 2 Peter 3:9). Therefore, through the work of the Holy Spirit, God draws all men to Himself, seeking to convict them of sin and bring them to repentance. Anybody who makes a free and well-informed decision to reject Christ thus seals his own fate; he is self-condemned. His damnation can't be blamed on God: on the contrary, he has resisted God's every effort to save him. He separates himself from God forever, in defiance of God's will that he be saved. In a sense, then, God doesn't send anybody to hell—people send themselves." –**William Craig**

"Tolerance used to be the attitude that we took toward one another when we disagreed about an important issue; we would agree to treat each other with respect, even though we refused to embrace each other's view on a particular topic. Tolerance is now the act of recognizing and embracing all views as equally valuable and true, even though they often make opposite truth claims." –**J. Warner Wallace**

"When someone makes an unbiblical claim, rather than immediately disagreeing with him and presenting my perspective, I like to ask a question or two to see if the person can support his claim with good arguments or evidence...My four favorite questions can be remembered with the simple acronym E.C.H.O...What *evidence* is there to support that? Can you *clarify* what you mean by that? *How* did you come to that conclusion? *Okay*, so what does that prove?...Asking friendly but probing questions can help a person see the weakness of a particular perspective. And he or she might then be more open to hearing your point of view on the subject." **-Charlie Campbell**

"The doctrine of the Trinity...is truth for the heart. The fact that it can not be satisfactorily explained, instead of being against it, is in its favor. Such a truth had to be revealed; no one could imagine it." **-A.W. Tozer**

"Historians point out that the basis of modern science depends on the assumption that the universe was made by a rational creator. An orderly universe makes perfect sense only if it were made by an orderly Creator. But if there is no creator, or if Zeus and his gang were in charge, why should there be any order at all? So, not only is a strong Christian belief not an obstacle to science, such a belief was its very foundation." **-Jonathan Sarfati**

"The philosophy of experimental science…began its discoveries and made use of its methods in the faith, not the knowledge, that it was dealing with a rational universe controlled by a creator who did not act upon whim nor interfere with the forces He had set in operation…It is surely one of the curious paradoxes of history that science, which professionally has little to do with faith, owes its origins to an act of faith that the universe can be rationally interpreted, and that science today is sustained by that assumption." **-Loren Eiseley**

"As an atheist...I concluded that there was no God based on what I thought to be good reasons...But when I started investigating Christianity, I began finding more and more evidence pointing away from atheism and toward belief in God." **-Lee Strobel**

"If you want truth to go round the world you must hire an express train to pull it, but if you want a lie to go round the world, it will fly; it is as light as a feather, and a breath will carry it. It is well said in the old Proverb, 'A lie will go round the world while truth is pulling its boots on.'" –**Charles Spurgeon**

"When someone claims that my belief that Jesus is the only way is intolerant and offensive, they ignore the fact that their pluralist approach is likewise intolerant and offensive. They are being intolerant of exclusivist views and offensive to those who hold them."
–**Michael Licona**

"When we read the New Testament, we see that credible historical reasons exist to support the resurrection of Christ, but many scholars refuse even to consider the evidence, for they are antecedently convinced that resurrections cannot happen. This fundamental bias, i.e., naturalistic philosophy, is all too often cloaked as "objective history."'" –**Thomas R. Schreiner**

"Gravity explains the motions of the planets, but it cannot explain who set the planets in motion. God governs all things and knows all that is or can be done." –**Isaac Newton**

"To say that we cannot know anything about God is to say something about God; it is to say that if there is a God, he is unknowable. But in that case, he is not *entirely* unknowable, for the agnostic certainly thinks that we can know one thing about him: That nothing *else* can be known about him." –**J. Budziszewski**

"Anyone trying to pass off a false resurrection story as the truth would never say the women were the first witnesses at the tomb. In the first century, a woman's testimony was not considered on par with that of a man. An invented story would say that the men—the brave men—had discovered the empty tomb. Yet all four Gospels say the women were the first witnesses while cowardly men had their doors locked for fear of the Jews." –**Frank Turek**

"The tragedy is that evolution is a nineteenth–century philosophy that has been destroyed by twentieth–century science. Yet the lie continues to be perpetrated, not on scientific grounds, but because it is what morally justifies our immoral society today." –**Ron Carlson**

"One response was given by the innkeeper when Mary and Joseph wanted to find a room where the Child could be born. The innkeeper was not hostile; he was not opposed to them, but his inn was crowded; his hands were full; his mind was preoccupied. This is the answer that millions are giving today. Like a Bethlehem innkeeper, they cannot find room for Christ. All the accommodations in their hearts are already taken up by other crowding interests. Their response is not atheism. It is not defiance. It is preoccupation and the feeling of being able to get on reasonably well without Christianity."
–Billy Graham

"If you were to force people to do something against their free choice, you would be dehumanizing them. The option of forcing everyone to go to heaven is immoral, because it's dehumanizing; it strips them of the dignity of making their own decision; it denies them their freedom of choice; and it treats them as a means to an end. When God allows people to say 'no' to him, he actually respects and dignifies them." **–J.P. Moreland**

"Therefore, when a person refuses to come to Christ it is never just because of lack of evidence or because of intellectual difficulties: at root, he refuses to come because he willingly ignores and rejects the drawing of God's Spirit on his heart. No one in the final analysis really fails to become a Christian because of lack of arguments; he fails to become a Christian because he loves darkness rather than light and wants nothing to do with God." **–William Craig**

"One of the reasons a person must turn to Jesus in order to be forgiven (and not some other person or deity) is because Jesus is the one we've sinned against. He's God. We can't invent gods and cry out to man–made deities and hope they will save us. These other gods don't even exist. They are inventions of men." **–Charlie Campbell**

Finding Peace with God

Do you know the loving, merciful God revealed to us in the Bible? Are you experiencing the peace that comes with knowing your sins have been forgiven and that all is right between you and God? You can.

That is why Jesus, God in the flesh, suffered and died on that cruel wooden cross two thousand years ago. He was paying the penalty for your sins so that you could be forgiven, escape eternity in Hell, and be brought back into a right relationship with God. He rose from the grave three days later and today offers all mankind:

- "the forgiveness of sins" (Acts 26:18)
- "peace with God" (Romans 5:1)
- the "free gift" of "everlasting life" (Romans 6:23; John 3:16)

That's great news friend! Everlasting life, forgiveness of all your sins, peace with God!? I don't know what you normally receive for Christmas, but this is way better! How do you receive that gift?

Jesus said, "Whosoever believes in Him will not perish but have everlasting life" (John 3:16). That's it! Jesus did all the work. All you need to do is place your faith in Him. And you can do that right now. God is a prayer away. You can pray something like this:

> God, thank You for loving me. I'm so sorry for my sins. I want to turn away from them. I renounce them! I believe Jesus died on the cross for my sins. So, please forgive me. Wash away my sins. I trust in Jesus Christ to save me. Come into my life. Be my Lord and Savior and make me into the person You want me to be. Amen!

The Bible says, "Whoever calls upon the name of the Lord will be saved" (Romans 10:13). So, if you have placed your faith in Jesus, God has forgiven you of your sins. The apostle John said, "These things I have written to you who believe in the name of the Son of God, so that you may know that you have eternal life" (1 John 5:13). Now begins an exciting new journey, walking with God.

To grow in your relationship with God...

A. Begin reading through the New Testament.

Get a good "study Bible." I recommend the *ESV Study Bible* or *The NKJV Study Bible*. These have helpful notes in them that will explain the historical context, meaning of passages, etc.

B. Start talking (praying) to God.

He loves you and wants to have a relationship with you. You can talk to Him about anything. "The prayer of the upright is His delight" (Proverbs 15:8).

C. Get connected to a conservative Bible-believing church where the Bible is trusted and studied in its entirety.

Check out the church's "Doctrinal Statement" or "Beliefs" on their website. If they don't clearly lay out their beliefs, stay away. The church should hold to doctrines similar to ours at alwaysbeready.com/abr-beliefs. These are held widely by Christian churches all over the world. If the church has a new believer's class, sign up to attend. Please steer clear of Mormon ("Latter Day Saints") and Jehovah's Witnesses churches. These groups claim to be Christian, but they espouse many unbiblical doctrines.

D. Make friends with other Christians.

It's important to find other Christians who can encourage you and be a blessing to you in your new relationship with Jesus. If you have friends or family members who are Christians, let them know of the decision you've made. They will rejoice and pray for you.

Let me know of your decision as well.
Email me at: **abr@alwaysbeready.com**

OWN 34 VIDEOS & AUDIO LECTURES BY CHARLIE CAMPBELL ON THIS WOOD FLASH DRIVE

Available at
AlwaysBeReady.com

AMAZINGLY...

this tiny USB flash drive contains the entire library of Charlie Campbell's videos (mp4s) and audio lectures (mp3s) on a wide range of apologetic issues. Just plug it into the USB port on your television or computer and begin watching or listening. You can also transfer the files to your iPad, iPhone, or other tablet (simple directions included). These videos and lectures will strengthen your faith in God and the Bible and equip you to answer atheists, skeptics, Muslims, Mormons, Jehovah's Witnesses, Hindus, Buddhists, New Agers, and others. Free shipping in the USA. Questions? Email us at: **ABR@AlwaysBeReady.com**.

WANT TO CONTINUE LEARNING? TAKE CHARLIE'S ONLINE COURSE.

If you enjoyed this book, you'll love Charlie Campbell's online apologetics course. All classes are on-demand videos that stream right to your device any time of day. Classes include: "Evidence for God," "Answering Atheists' Objections to God and the Bible," "Why Does God Allow Evil and Suffering?" And others. Learn more and watch a sample class at:

AlwaysBeReady.Teachable.com
Oh, and no homework or tests—just fun times of learning!

Index

1 Corinthians
  13:1 89
  15:6 68
  15:13–17 100
1 John
  4:1 21
  5:13 106
1 Kings
  18:38 94
1 Peter
  3:15 21, 37
1 Samuel
  1:19–20 72
1 Thessalonians
  5 75
  5:21 7
1 Timothy
  2:4 102
  3:15 35
  4:1 21
  6:6–10 82
2 Corinthians
  5:20 89
  10:4–5 26, 37
  12:9 82
2 Peter
  3:7 28
  3:9 102
2 Thessalonians
  1:9 91
2 Timothy
  2:24–25 18
  2:24–26 37
  3:16 23, 53
  4:7 54

A

Abel 60
abortion 14, 47, 50, 59, 72, 101
Abraham 9, 30, 58, 60, 92, 94
Abraham Lincoln 9
absolutes 17
Acts 40
  1:2–3 71
  4:16–17 101
  9 50
  17:26 63
  26:8 99
  26:18 106
Adam 72, 73, 86, 92
Adolf Hitler 36, 90
adultery 59, 101
age of the earth 86
agnostics 5, 14
Alan Redpath 98
Alan Sheldon 96
Alan Shlemon 31, 58, 80
Albert Cummins 47
Albert Einstein 19, 21
Albert Mohler 17, 45, 77
alcoholism 29, 32, 53
Alexander 14, 16, 86, 92
Alex McFarland 29, 40, 60
aliens 74
Alister McGrath 20, 35, 36, 42
Allah 96
Allan Sandage 53
alphabet 57, 75
Americans 77, 93, 98
amoeba 64
anatomy 63
Andrew Snelling 22
Andrew Wilson 24
Andy Bannister 7, 16, 18, 24, 33, 46, 69, 72
angels 50, 61
Anselm 84
Antonin Scalia 40
Antony Flew 39, 63, 83
anvil 12
apes 81
Apocrypha 27, 28
apologetics 2, 7, 8, 13, 14, 19, 26, 31, 42, 89, 99
apologists 18, 35, 73, 89
apostasy 67, 68

apostasy 67
archaeology 8, 16, 18, 20, 24, 27, 30, 32, 40, 47, 79, 99
arguments 16, 17, 18, 19, 21, 22, 26, 29, 30, 31, 35, 36, 38, 41, 42, 55, 56, 59, 68, 69, 81, 82, 83, 95, 99, 102, 105
Ariel Roth 53
Aristotle 70
Ark, Noah's 39
army 87, 88, 95
art 85, 87
astrology 26, 27
astronomers 27, 77
astronomy 77, 80
atheism 8, 22, 33, 35, 36, 37, 42, 47, 50, 60, 63, 85, 89, 97, 103, 105
atheist 9, 11, 18, 35, 36, 39, 44, 49, 53, 54, 62, 71, 72, 75, 82, 90, 99, 103
atheists 3, 5, 13, 14, 16, 18, 20, 22, 28, 36, 39, 48, 50, 54, 55, 59, 61, 74, 89, 102, 109
atmospheric circulation 29
atoms 34, 77, 79
Augustine 67, 84
A.W. Tozer 103

B

bacteria 55
Bathsheba 101
beginning of the universe 38, 45, 76, 86
beginning of universe 14, 101
Ben Hobrink 52, 63
Benjamin Wiker 98
Bernard Ramm 86
Bertrand Russell 45

Bethlehem 85, 105
betting that God exists 80
Bible's transforming power 29, 37, 52
Big Bang 79
bigotry 32, 80
Bill Gates 88
Bill Maher 73
Billy Graham 76, 105
biochemists 56
biologists 56
biology 56, 57, 74, 75, 80, 84, 94
birds 39
Blaise Pascal 80, 85
blind 28, 70, 73, 76, 83, 84, 86
blind faith 73, 83
blood 29, 34, 95
Bob Hoekstra 18, 82
boldness 36
bones 20, 34, 86
Book of Mormon 16, 43, 55, 57, 83, 99
Brahma 96
brain 34, 47, 56, 95
bread 23, 49, 85
Brett Kunkle 26
Brian Edwards 43
Brian Thomas 94
Brooke Westcott 86
Buddha 8, 17, 22, 23, 69, 92, 96
Buddhism 23, 43
Burk Parsons 12

C

Caesar 14, 16, 47, 86
Cal Thomas 9
Canaanites 18, 20
canon of Scripture 27, 52
capitalism 85
Carnegie Simpson 92
carpenter 88
Catholicism 27, 28
cells 34, 37, 47, 53, 56, 57, 59, 62, 79, 80, 90, 94
chance 10, 39, 40, 52, 63, 71, 76, 90

chaos 8
Charlemagne 14
Charles Colson 8, 10, 37, 47
Charles Darwin 5, 31, 35, 37, 59, 64, 68, 69, 70, 76, 77
   referring to himself as a theist 76
Charles Ryrie 23, 92
Charles Spurgeon 8, 17, 21, 29, 38, 44, 54, 66, 80, 83, 104
Charles Swindoll 12, 15
Charles the Great 92
Charlie Campbell 5, 8, 10, 13, 16, 20, 23, 25, 28, 31, 34, 37, 44, 51, 54, 58, 59, 61, 64, 67, 69, 72, 75, 78, 83, 86, 89, 91, 94, 97, 99, 101, 103, 105, 109, 110
chemistry 84
children 56, 57, 61, 66, 72, 93
China 52, 77
Christianity 3, 7, 9, 10, 11, 12, 13, 16, 17, 18, 19, 22, 23, 26, 29, 33, 35, 38, 41, 43, 50, 54, 60, 62, 65, 72, 76, 80, 82, 87, 88, 89, 90, 98, 99, 100, 103, 105
Christopher Hitchens 21, 24, 28
church 19, 25, 26, 31, 35, 37, 39, 40, 44, 45, 48, 52, 54, 67, 68, 81, 83, 89, 93, 107
churches 11, 28, 68, 107
Clement of Alexandria 94
clouds 101
coins 57
Colin Patterson 51, 52
Colin Smith 67
Colossians
  2:8 27
comets 87

common sense 40, 58, 84
complexity 37, 39, 52, 53, 56, 59, 70, 74, 79, 90, 101
Confucianism 43
Confucius 8, 22, 92, 96
conscience 8, 83, 97
Constantine 41
constants in the universe 101
contentment 82
continents 22, 101
"contradictions" in the Bible 9, 20, 33
conversion 52, 65, 87
correction 64, 80
cosmologists 69
cosmology 80
cosmos 11, 27
Council of Nicaea 93
counterfeit 15, 95
counterfeits 21
Craig Hazen 73
creed 54
criminal 78
cross 106
crucifixion 54, 61, 62, 88, 98
Crusades 36
crutch 50, 85
C.S. Lewis 9, 13, 15, 18, 24, 30, 35, 41, 46, 55, 65, 77, 83, 91, 96
cults 34, 39, 72
Cults 12, 54
culture 7, 8, 19, 32, 36, 45, 59, 96, 97
curse 25, 72, 73
cyanide 72
Czeslaw Milosz 94

D

Daniel
  2 50
  4:5 50
  4:35 50
  7 50
  9:24–27 60
  10:12–13 61

10:20 61
Dan Story 26, 52
darkness 48, 54, 78, 89, 91, 97, 105
Darwinism 8, 56, 65, 66, 77, 88, 98
Darwinists 11, 35, 65, 98
Dave Hunt 57, 79
Dave Sterrett 16
David 30, 60, 70, 78, 90, 99, 101
David Marshall 60
Dead Sea Scrolls 58, 67
death 14, 15, 22, 26, 33, 39, 42, 51, 54, 58, 59, 61, 62, 73, 76, 77, 79, 83, 88, 94, 100, 101
deity of Christ 93
Dennis Prager 10
denomination 40, 77
denominations 67, 68
Derek Rishmawy 36
Deuteronomy
  8:3 23
  25:6 72
devil 26, 41
Devin Sena 50
Dinesh D'Souza 23, 37, 53, 60, 65, 87
disciples 26, 37, 42, 61, 62, 68, 69, 71, 78, 79, 93, 95, 100
disciples, martyrdom 10, 26, 49, 62, 77, 79, 100
D. James Kennedy 85
DNA 11, 19, 34, 39, 57, 64, 75, 79, 83, 87, 94
doctrine 8, 28, 34, 39, 43, 44, 51, 62, 63, 72, 74, 75, 77, 82, 98, 103
dog 42, 80
Donald Page 13
Don Stewart 84
door 85, 102
drugs 29
Dwight L. Moody 18

E

Earth 5, 9, 14, 16, 25, 27, 28, 34, 38, 47, 55, 57, 58, 59, 62, 63, 81, 82, 86, 88, 90, 94, 99
earthquakes 58, 62
Ecclesiastes
  1:6 29
  1:7 28
E.C.H.O. acronym 102
ecosystem 62
Ed Decker 11, 81
Ed Hindson 11
Ed Strauss 41
education 85
Edwin Yamauchi 81
Egypt 12
Elijah 60
Elisha 60
E.M. Blaiklock 76
Encyclopedia Britannica 11, 64, 74
entropy 28
E. Paul Hovey 9
Ephesians
  2:8-9 46
  4:15 18
  6:5-9 93
Ergun Caner 57
Eric Metaxas 39, 66
error 21, 34, 37, 43, 44, 57, 66, 68
Erwin Lutzer 68
eternity 23, 46, 99
evangelism 14, 28, 31, 67
evangelists 39
evaporation 101
Eve 72, 86, 92
evidence 3, 5, 7, 8, 12, 15, 16, 18, 23, 27, 28, 30, 31, 32, 33, 35, 41, 47, 48, 50, 53, 57, 58, 60, 61, 63, 65, 68, 70, 71, 73, 76, 77, 78, 79, 80, 86, 92, 93, 96, 97, 98, 99, 100, 102, 103, 104, 105

evil 3, 11, 18, 19, 21, 22, 25, 29, 30, 36, 40, 54, 58, 59, 61, 62, 76, 82, 83, 89, 97, 99
evolution 3, 8, 13, 19, 41, 51, 52, 56, 60, 61, 63, 64, 65, 66, 68, 70, 72, 77, 81, 84, 86, 88, 94, 104
  intermediate links 30
evolutionists 9, 51, 55, 63
experiences 16, 33, 40, 48, 67, 79, 81, 83, 84, 90
extra-terrestrial intelligence 16
eyes 28, 34, 52, 64, 75

F

fairy story 74
faith 12, 13, 16, 18, 19, 20, 21, 24, 26, 29, 31, 38, 39, 40, 42, 44, 47, 48, 51, 54, 55, 58, 64, 66, 67, 70, 71, 73, 79, 82, 83, 84, 86, 93, 97, 100, 103, 106, 109
faith to be an atheist 54
false teachers 45
false teachings 15, 67, 74
Father, God as our 57
fear 27, 29, 36, 48, 64, 104
feelings 72
F.F. Bruce 52, 65
finely-tuned conditions 13, 31, 69, 101
fishermen 66
Flavius Josephus 25, 50, 61
  mention of Jesus 61
Flood 39, 52, 75, 92
floods 62
food 82, 95
force, a spiritual 96
forgiveness 31
fossil record 41, 51, 61, 63, 70
fossils 22, 41, 61, 63, 70, 77, 86
Francis Bacon 85

Francis Collins 101
Francis Crick 74
Franklin Graham 15
Frank Turek 11, 18, 22, 27, 32, 36, 38, 46, 49, 51, 56, 59, 62, 64, 68, 74, 77, 80, 84, 89, 90, 97, 99, 101, 104
Fred Hoyle 69, 74, 84, 90
freedom 19, 64, 93, 101, 105
free will 30, 64, 105
friendship 78, 90
Fritz Ridenour 10
frog 81
fruit 101
fulfilled prophecies 8, 10, 16, 23, 60, 83

G

galaxies 99
Galileo Galilei 73, 84
Gary Habermas 10, 62, 100
G.B. Hardy 22
G. Campbell Morgan 44
Genesis 14, 20, 72
  1:1 14, 87, 99
  2:1 86
  3 83
  7:20 39
  9:5-6 63
  29:33 72
genetic programming 59
geological formation 30
geology 30, 75, 90
George Sim Johnson 11
Germany 89
G.K. Chesterton 9, 12, 55, 98
Glen Scrivener 11
Gnostic Gospels 87
God
  why not just appear to us? 28
gods 17, 18, 27, 53, 63, 105
Goethe 92
Gomorrah 60

good health 80
gospel 3, 18, 23, 28, 31, 34, 36, 37, 41, 43, 45, 49, 50, 52, 62, 66, 67, 68, 74, 81, 82, 85, 87
Gospels 19, 46, 60, 81, 87, 91, 104
  when were they completed? 81
Gottfried Leibniz 85
government 77, 85
grace 46, 48, 62, 82
Grand Canyon 22
gravitational field 29
gravity 104
greed 25, 91, 94
greediness 82
Greg Bahnsen 25
Greg Koukl 7, 12, 16, 24, 33, 43, 50, 55, 62, 67, 68, 79, 82, 88, 93
gun control 81

H

hammers 12
Hank Hanegraaff 45, 72
happiness 11, 50, 58
health and wealth heresy 82
heart 20, 22, 28, 34, 44, 48, 50, 56, 61
heartbeat 55
Heaven 4, 24, 31, 50, 65, 67, 82, 94, 96, 105
Hebrews
  4:12 50
  13:8 45
Hell 3, 4, 24, 41, 62, 67, 75, 89, 90, 91, 94, 96, 102, 106
Henry Morris 21, 75, 86
Henry Schaefer 38
Henry Van Dyke 78
Herbert Spencer 14
heresy 9
heretic 12
H.G. Wells 85
hiddeness of God 64, 77
Himalayas 22, 52, 69

Hinduism 17
Hindu Vedas 16
historians 25, 32, 40, 46, 50, 76, 85, 103
history 7, 8, 9, 15, 16, 18, 20, 23, 24, 27, 29, 31, 32, 33, 37, 40, 44, 46, 47, 49, 52, 58, 60, 70, 71, 72, 73, 75, 76, 79, 81, 83, 85, 87, 88, 89, 90, 91, 92, 94, 98, 100, 103, 104, 107
Hittites 30
H.L. Hastings 12
holiness 45, 80, 86, 95
Holy Spirit 56, 102
homosexuality 26, 32
Hosea
  1:1 50
hostility 31, 42
human beings, complexity of 20, 53
human nature 20, 92
human reason 46
humility 18, 37, 39
hydrological cycle 28, 100

I

Ignatius 93
illness 80, 94
inerrancy 74
infinite knowledge 11, 33
Inquisition 36
insecticide resistance 65
inspired, Scripture is 11, 12, 15, 19, 20, 23, 27, 29, 30, 43, 45, 52, 53, 54, 88, 98
intellectual pacifism 95
intelligence 11, 16, 34, 41, 44, 57, 62, 98
intelligent design 9, 13, 44, 80, 83, 84, 85, 90
intermediate links 30
interpretation, Bible 33, 84, 98
intolerance 12, 32, 69, 70, 74, 102, 104
intuition 84

inventing religions 13
Iraq 82
Irenaeus 94
Isaac 60
Isaac Newton 9, 45, 63, 85, 87, 100, 104
Isaiah
  9:6 93
  40:22 28
Islam 15, 23, 43, 64, 65, 66, 69
island 93
Israel 40, 60
itinerant preacher 88

J
Jacob 60
James Boice 30
Java man 13
J. Budziszewski 104
J.C. Ryle 12, 20, 30, 49, 56, 57
J.D. Greaar 90
Jeffrey Russell 39, 80, 101
Jeffrey Tomkins 19, 47
Jehovah's Witnesses 93, 107, 109
Jeremiah 28, 36, 37
  1:9–10 36
  33:22 28
Jerome Lejeune 66
Jerusalem 38, 60, 81
Jesus 2, 3, 8, 9, 10, 11, 14, 15, 16, 17, 19, 21, 22, 23, 24, 25, 26, 27, 28, 29, 31, 32, 33, 37, 38, 40, 41, 42, 43, 44, 45, 46, 53, 54, 56, 58, 59, 60, 61, 62, 65, 66, 67, 68, 69, 70, 71, 72, 73, 74, 75, 76, 78, 79, 80, 81, 83, 85, 86, 87, 88, 89, 90, 91, 92, 93, 94, 95, 96, 97, 98, 99, 100, 101, 102, 104, 105, 106, 107
  high view of Scripture 23, 92, 98
  liar, lunatic, or Lord 41
  mentioned outside Bible 25, 81
  miracles 28
  only way of salvation 9, 94, 104, 105
  virgin birth 11, 38, 83
Job
  26:7 29
John 87
  3:16 106
  3:19 97
  6:1–66 94
  7:17 75
  7:46 68
  8:32 21
  8:58 92, 93
  14:6 65, 80, 85
  14:11 70
  20:28 93
John Ankerberg 74
John Calvin 42
John Elder 32
John Lennox 12, 16, 21, 41, 50, 63, 74, 75, 84, 97, 100
John Locke 85
John MacArthur 11, 14, 22, 28, 31, 35, 49, 53, 54, 66, 68, 75, 84, 86, 100
John Piper 54
John Stott 14
John Walvoord 15, 29, 62, 74, 81
John Warwick Montgomery 56, 81
Jonah 38, 60, 92
Jonathan Sarfati 103
Jonathan Wells 80, 98
Joseph of Arimathea 79
Joseph Smith 17, 69
Joseph Stalin 36
Josephus, Flavius 25, 50, 61;
  mention of Jesus 61
Josh McDowell 8, 16, 22, 32, 40, 43, 46, 53, 66, 80, 97, 100
joy 30
J.P. Moreland 42, 64, 95, 105
J. Sidlow Baxter 85
Judaism 23
Judas 87
Jude
  1:3 21, 86
judging 12, 17, 32, 33
judgment 94
judgmental 12, 32, 33
Julius Caesar 16
Justin Martyr 93
J. Vernon McGee 10, 34
J. Warner Wallace 19, 64, 71, 102

K
Karl Marx 35
Keith Green 52
Keith Ward 89
Ken Ham 19, 39, 73
Kevin DeYoung 36, 60, 98

L
lack of evidence 105
Landon Schott 26
Larry Hatfield 89
Las Vegas 81
Latter Day Saints 107
lawgiver 17, 60, 71, 79
law of conservation of mass and energy 28
laws of the universe 69
LDS 107
Lee Strobel 8, 14, 21, 26, 28, 40, 47, 57, 65, 76, 99, 103
legends 46
legislating morality 80
Leviticus
  17:11 29
Lewis Sperry Chafer 9
liberal theologians 30
light 33, 38, 42, 49, 53, 54, 63, 64, 78, 85, 86, 89, 90, 97, 103, 105
Linus Pauling 53
listening 43, 63, 93

115

lives change for the good 32
logic 14, 17, 38, 39, 40, 66, 71, 76, 84, 89, 95
London 35, 69
Loren Eiseley 103
love 3, 4, 7, 14, 16, 18, 20, 25, 26, 30, 31, 32, 37, 45, 62, 63, 64, 66, 71, 74, 75, 78, 79, 82, 86, 89, 90, 98
Lucy fossil 13
Luke 40, 87, 91, 101
  9:20 43
  16:23 91
  16:24 91
  16:27–31 95
  17:26–29 92
  17:28–29 92
lunatic 41, 96
lying 25, 42, 99, 101

M

Mace Baker 81
Malcolm Muggeridge 58
manna 60
manuscript evidence 31
manuscripts 51, 67
Mao 36
Mark 87
  10:6–8 92
Mark Mittelberg 7, 76, 79
Mars 55
Martin Luther 97
martyrs 95, 100
Mary 59, 87, 105
materialism 22, 35, 77, 102
mathematics 13, 84, 101
Matthew 87, 101
  4:4 23
  7:15 21
  8:12 91
  9:9 43
  10:15 92
  12:40 92
  13:42 91
  13:50 91
  18:10 61
  19:3–5 92
  19:4 72
  24:38–39 92
  25:30 91
  25:46 91
  28:6 99
  28:18–20 50
Matt Slick 25
Matt Smethurst 45
meaning 17, 19, 42, 74, 83, 84, 88, 101, 107
Medina 69
meteors 58
Michael Behe 35, 37
Michael Bird 83
Michael Denton 44
Michael Licona 104
microscope 72
Millar Burrows 16, 30
Millennials 19
minds 22, 55, 56, 58, 73, 80, 84, 86, 93
miracles 11, 17, 23, 32, 38, 49, 53, 60, 63, 66, 71, 91, 92, 94, 95
missiles 78
missions agencies 67
molecules 97
money 82, 86
  love of money 82
monkeys 71
moon 58
morality 33, 42, 80, 88, 97
moral law 71, 79, 101
Mormon Church 107
Mormons 16, 43, 55, 57, 83, 99, 107
Moses 17, 20, 23, 60, 72
mountains 39, 52, 55, 57, 58
Mount Rushmore 20
Muhammad 8, 17, 22, 23, 69, 86, 92, 95, 96
murder 25, 60, 78, 94, 98, 101
muscles 20, 34
Museum of Natural History 51

music 85
Muslim apologists 95
Muslims 65, 66, 109;
  also see: Islam
mutations 20, 39, 72
mystery religions 33
myth 19, 43, 45, 98

N

Naaman 60
Nancy Pearcey 93, 97
nanomachinery 62
Napoleon Bonaparte I 14, 86, 92
narrow-minded 32
Nathan Busenitz 48
National Geographic Society 99
natural selection 8, 64, 65, 70
nature 57
navies 88
Nazareth 46, 85, 86
Neanderthal man 13
Nebraska man 13
Nelson Glueck 24
New Testament 25, 27, 33, 44, 51, 52, 57, 65, 75, 77, 81, 82, 91, 104, 107
Nicaea 93
Nicolaus Copernicus 84
Nietzsche 87
Noah 39, 60, 92
non-essentials 71
nonsense 41, 50
Norman Geisler 8, 15, 17, 21, 25, 33, 35, 45, 50, 60, 71, 77, 85, 90, 92, 95, 99
North Korea 89
nothing 8, 14, 49, 54, 55, 68, 86, 93, 99
nothingness 94
Numbers
  16:31–33 94
  16:35 94
numismatics 30

O

objective standard 71
objective truth 17
occult 54
ocean 101
Old Testament 10, 23, 25, 27, 40, 44, 50, 58, 92, 93
omnipotence 13
one solitary life 88
only way of salvation, Jesus 9, 94, 104, 105
open mind 12
opium 94
Oprah Winfrey 17
oral tradition 81
Os Guinness 31, 44

P

pagans 33, 34, 37, 54, 63
paleontology 52, 61
panspermia 74
pantheism 96
parallels between Christianity and other religions 34
pastors 39, 72
patience 25, 37
Paul Brand 34
Paul Copan 30, 70
Paul Davies 31, 69, 85
Paul Little 24
Paul Maier 27, 79
Paul, the apostle 35, 37, 42, 54, 56, 63, 68, 82, 98, 99, 100
Peking man 13
persecution 12, 49
Peter 68, 87, 91
Peter Kreeft 12, 19, 46, 49, 71, 96
pharoahs 47
Philippians
 1:7 21
Philip Schaff 40, 87
Philip Yancey 34
Phillip E. Johnson 35, 57, 69, 77
philosophy 29, 35, 43, 49, 55, 69, 103, 104
physicists 69, 85
physics 69, 80, 84
Piltdown man 13
plane crash 58
planets 9, 27, 54, 74, 77, 87, 104
plate tectonics 62
Plato 70
plenary inspiration 19, 23, 88;
 also see: inspired
police 78
pollution 25
Pontius Pilate 61
popes 97
postmodernism 95
power 10, 13, 19, 27, 29, 35, 37, 47, 49, 55, 66, 86
preaching apologetically 36
pride 25
Princeton's Institute for Advanced Science 13
prophecies 8, 10, 16, 23, 40, 60
prospering 80
prostitution 101
protoplasm 59
Proverbs
 15:8 107
Psalm
 14:1 11
 36:9 94
 102:25–27 29
 119:130 50
 127:3 72
punishment 26, 62, 91, 96
pyramids 12, 47

Q

questions to ask skeptics 102
Quran 16, 53, 55, 57, 95
 errors in the Quran 57

R

races 63
Rahab 101
rain 20, 101
Randall Price 58
Randomness 8
random variation 65
Randy Alcorn 13, 33, 40, 47, 59, 61, 75, 95, 101
Randy Guliuzza 47
rape 25, 101
R.A. Torrey 30, 48, 56
Ravi Zacharias 11, 23, 29, 33, 42, 47, 51, 59, 68, 71, 74, 96
Ray Comfort 55, 67, 86, 93
R.C. Sproul 18, 29, 73
reincarnation 55
relativism 17, 45, 97, 101
relativists 12
religion 10, 11, 21, 22, 23, 24, 42, 43, 57, 60, 63, 64, 65, 70, 76, 77, 79, 81, 87, 94, 95, 98
religions 9, 13, 18, 22, 24, 32, 33, 38, 43, 54, 60, 76, 77, 89, 98, 101
 inventing 13
religious leaders 24, 65
religious pluralism 76
Rene Descartes 85
repentance 18, 20, 37, 102
resurrection 10, 15, 22, 23, 26, 33, 36, 37, 38, 42, 49, 56, 61, 63, 66, 68, 69, 71, 76, 77, 78, 79, 83, 86, 98, 99, 100, 104, 106
 stolen body theory 21
Revelation
 14:6 50
 19:20 91
Richard Dawkins 28, 35, 64, 68, 74, 97
Richard Lewontin 102
Rick Oliver 72
rivers 57

RNA 19
Robert Jastrow 27, 55
Robert Laidlaw 46
Robert Velarde 18, 49
rock layers 22
Roman Empire 41, 66
Romans
 1:24–32 59
 5:1 106
 6:23 106
 10:13 106
 10:14–17 50
 12:2 33
Rome 37, 47
Ronald Nash 34, 82
Ronald Reagan 14
Ronald Tacelli 46
Ronald Wright 27
Ron Carlson 11, 81, 104
Ron Rhodes 7, 13, 17, 27, 43, 52, 73, 89, 93
Russia 89
Ryan Snuffer 71

S

salt 101
salvation 29, 43, 46, 48, 73, 100;
 only through Jesus 9, 94, 104, 105
sand 75
Satan 27
satellite 59
scholars 8, 18, 34, 51, 61, 73, 99, 104
science 7, 9, 10, 13, 14, 15, 20, 21, 27, 28, 29, 32, 35, 37, 38, 41, 47, 49, 53, 55, 57, 59, 64, 69, 76, 78, 80, 81, 84, 85, 86, 89, 90, 93, 98, 100, 101, 102, 103, 104
scientists 9, 14, 22, 28, 37, 38, 49, 50, 55, 59, 69, 77, 84, 88, 94
Scott Hahn 98
Sean McDowell 17, 25, 72, 87
secular schools 93
seeds 27, 74, 101
self–defeating arguments 17
selfishness 25
seminaries 54, 67
serpent 60
Shakespeare, William 26
sheep 56, 80
shellfish 22
shepherd 56, 80
sickness 80
Siddhartha Guatama 69
Sigmund Freud 35
similarities between Christianity and other religions 34
Simon Greenleaf 88, 100
sin 8, 19, 38, 82, 91, 96, 102
skepticism 14, 30, 48, 92
slavery 3, 25, 85, 93, 101
soap 76
Socrates 16, 96
Sodom 39, 60, 92
solar system 63, 77
Solomon 60
Soren Kierkegaard 85
Soviet Union 69
species 8, 70
spiritual journey 99
stars 27, 28, 54, 58, 61
Stephen Hawking 74
Stephen Jay Gould 61
Steven Lawson 38, 74, 94
struggling with faith 48
submarines 59, 78
Sue Bohlin 82
Suetonius 25
suffering 3, 10, 11, 13, 29, 39, 40, 58, 61, 78, 82, 83, 94
sun 12, 18, 34, 38, 54, 55, 57, 63, 87, 100
supernatural 16, 20, 27, 30, 53, 54, 86
superstition 56

T

Tacitus 25
Talmud 19, 25
Tamar 101
tares 34
teachers 39, 45, 91, 93
technology 21, 62
telescope 59
temptation 82, 85
Ten Commandments 63
Tertullian 54
textbooks 61, 63
text of Bible accurately transmitted 50, 51;
 also see: Dead Sea Scrolls; Manuscripts
theologians 30, 55, 84
theology 5, 54, 77
Thomas 87
Thomas Aquinas 84
Thomas Arnold 71
Thomas R. Schreiner 104
thorn 82
TIME Magazine 15
Tim Keller 9, 16, 20, 41, 63, 70, 91
Timothy 37
tolerance 12, 32, 69, 70, 74, 102, 104
Tom Stoppard 85
transitional fossils 52, 61
translations 58
tribulation 80
Trinity 46, 103
truth 10, 11, 17, 18, 19, 21, 25, 26, 35, 37, 38, 40, 42, 44, 45, 52, 53, 65, 67, 68, 69, 71, 73, 75, 80, 81, 85, 93, 95, 96, 97, 98, 99, 102, 103, 104
tsunami 13
Tylenol 72
tyranny 101

U

unborn child 47
unity 71, 74, 75
unity of Scripture 15, 46, 52, 64
universe 9, 13, 14, 27, 31, 32, 34, 38, 39, 45, 54, 59, 62, 69, 71, 76, 79, 85, 86, 89, 90, 95, 97, 98, 99, 101, 103
University of Chicago 51
unseen 61, 84

V

vegetables 101
veins 34
Vietnam 89
virgin birth 11, 38, 83
Voltaire 51

W

Walter Bradley 9
Walter Brown 42
Walter Kaiser 92
Walter Martin 39, 54
water 13, 38, 61
water cycle 100, 101
Watergate 10
W.E. Sangster 83
Westminster Abbey 69
W.F. Albright 58
Will Durant 91
William Craig 7, 15, 23, 42, 48, 58, 77, 78, 102, 105
William Dembski 65
William Kelvin 84
William Lane Craig 7, 15, 23, 48, 58, 77, 78, 105
William Lecky 60
William Shakespeare 26
wind 101
wisdom 13, 26, 29, 92
witch burnings 36
witnessing 31, 43, 87, 94
womb 15, 56, 59, 72
women 50, 59, 85, 104
worldview 11, 29, 42, 82, 97

Z

Zechariah 60
Zeus 96, 103
Zodiac signs 27

Characteristics of a God-Glorifying Ambassador of Jesus Christ

1. Loving.
"Watch, stand fast in the faith, be brave, be strong. Let all that you do be done with love." (1 Corinthians 16:13–14)

2. Ready, but gentle and respectful.
"Always be ready to give a defense to everyone who asks you a reason for the hope that is in you, yet do it with gentleness and respect..." (1 Peter 3:15)

3. Gracious.
"Let your speech always be with grace, seasoned with salt..." (Colossians 4:6)

4. Patient.
"And a servant of the Lord must not quarrel but be gentle to all, able to teach, patient, in humility correcting those who are in opposition..." (2 Timothy 2:24–26)

5. Humble.
"So then neither the one who plants nor the one who waters is anything, but God who causes the growth." (1 Corinthians 3:7)

6. Discerning.
"Do not give what is holy to the dogs; nor cast your pearls before swine, lest they trample them under their feet, and turn and tear you in pieces." (Matthew 7:6)

7. Obedient to Jesus's Great Commission.
"Go therefore and make disciples of all the nations, baptizing them in the name of the Father and of the Son and of the Holy Spirit, teaching them to observe all things that I have commanded you; and lo, I am with you always, even to the end of the age. Amen." (Matthew 28:19–20)

Made in the USA
Las Vegas, NV
13 January 2021